# Everyday Mathematics®

## The University of Chicago School Mathematics Project

# Differentiation Handbook

Grade **1**

Mc Graw Hill **Wright Group**

The **McGraw·Hill** Companies

## The University of Chicago School Mathematics Project (UCSMP)

Max Bell, Director, UCSMP Elementary Materials Component;
   Director, *Everyday Mathematics* First Edition
James McBride, Director, *Everyday Mathematics* Second Edition
Andy Isaacs, Director, *Everyday Mathematics* Third Edition
Amy Dillard, Associate Director, *Everyday Mathematics* Third Edition

### Authors
Amy Dillard
Kathleen Pitvorec

### Differentiation Assistant
Serena Hohmann

### Technical Art
Diana Barrie

### ELL Consultant
Kathryn B. Chval

### Photo Credits
©Ralph A. Clevenger/Corbis, cover, *center*; Ed-Imaging, pp. 10 *top*, 33 *top right*; ©Getty Images, cover, *bottom left*; ©Image DJ/Alamy, p. 9 *bottom middle*; ©Tom & Dee Ann McCarthy/Corbis, cover, *right*; ©Barrie Rokeach/Alamy, p. 9 *bottom left*; ©Swerve/Alamy, p. 9 *bottom right*.

### Permissions
Carl Sagan quotation 9806 from Dictionary of Quotations Third Edition, Newly Revised, reproduced by kind permission of Wordsworth Editions, LTD.

Deciding to Teach Them All, Tomlinson, C., Educational Leadership 61(2), © 2003, reprinted by permission. The Association for Supervision and Curriculum Development is a worldwide community of educators advocating sound policies and sharing best practices to achieve the success of each learner. To learn more, visit ASCD at www.ascd.org.

Gregory, G., Differentiated Instructional Strategies in Practice, p. 27, © 2003 by Corwin Press Inc., reprinted by permission of Corwin Press Inc.

## www.WrightGroup.com

 **Wright Group**

Send all inquiries to:
Wright Group/McGraw-Hill
P.O. Box 812960
Chicago, IL 60681

ISBN 0-07-604548-X

6 7 8 9 MAL 12 11 10 09 08 07

*The McGraw-Hill Companies*

# Contents

# Differentiating Instruction with *Everyday Mathematics*®

## Philosophy

> *Differentiation is a philosophy that enables teachers to plan strategically in order to reach the needs of the diverse learners in classrooms today.*
>
> (Gregory 2003, 27)

This handbook is intended as a guide to help you use *Everyday Mathematics* to provide differentiated mathematics instruction. A differentiated classroom is a rich learning environment that provides children with multiple avenues for acquiring content, making sense of ideas, developing skills, and demonstrating what they know.

In this sense, differentiated instruction is synonymous with good teaching. Many experienced teachers differentiate instruction intuitively, making continual adjustments to meet the varying needs of individual children. By adapting instruction, teachers provide all children opportunities to engage in lesson content and to learn.

Though children follow different routes to success and acquire concepts and skills at different times, the philosophy of *Everyday Mathematics* is that all children should be expected to achieve high standards in their mathematics education, reaching the Grade-Level Goals in *Everyday Mathematics* and the benchmarks established in district and state standards.

*Everyday Mathematics* is an ideal curriculum for differentiating instruction for a variety of reasons. The *Everyday Mathematics* program:

◆ begins with an appreciation of the mathematical sensibilities that children bring with them to the classroom and connects to children's prior interests and experiences;

◆ incorporates predictable routines that help engage children in mathematics and regular practice in a variety of contexts;

◆ provides many opportunities throughout the year for children to acquire, process, and express mathematical concepts in concrete, pictorial, and symbolic ways;

◆ extends children's thinking about mathematical ideas through questioning that leads to deepened understandings of concepts;

- incorporates and validates a variety of learning strategies;

- emphasizes the process of problem solving as well as finding solutions;

- provides suggestions for enhancing or supporting children's learning in each lesson;

- encourages collaborative and cooperative groupings in addition to individual and whole-class work;

- facilitates the development and use of mathematical language and promotes academic discourse;

- provides teachers with information about the learning trajectories or paths to achieving Grade-Level Goals;

- highlights opportunities for teachers to assess children in multiple ways over time;

- suggests how children can demonstrate what they know in a variety of ways; and

- encourages children to reflect on their own strengths and weaknesses.

The purpose of this handbook is to provide ideas and strategies for differentiating instruction when using *Everyday Mathematics*. This handbook highlights differentiation that is embedded in the program and also points to features that can be readily adapted for individual children. The information and suggestions will help you use *Everyday Mathematics* to meet the needs of all learners—learners who need support in developing concepts, learners who need support in developing language proficiency, and learners who are ready to extend their mathematical knowledge and skills.

This handbook includes the following:

- a lesson overview to highlight the features that support differentiated instruction;

- general differentiation strategies and ideas for developing vocabulary, playing games, and using Math Boxes, as well as suggestions for how to implement the lessons to differentiate instruction effectively;

- specific ideas for differentiating the content of each unit, including suggestions for supporting vocabulary and adjusting the level of games; and

- a variety of masters that can be used to address the needs of individual learners.

# A Lesson Overview

*Everyday Mathematics* lessons are designed to accommodate a wide range of academic abilities and learning styles. This lesson overview highlights some of the strategies and opportunities for differentiating instruction that are incorporated into the lessons.

## 4·3 Comparing and Ordering Decimals

**Objective** To guide students as they compare and order decimals in tenths and hundredths.

### 1 Teaching the Lesson | materials

**Key Activities**
Students compare decimals using base-10 blocks. They append zeros to decimals in order to compare them. Then they put sets of decimals in sequential order.

*Math Journal 1*, pp. 82 and 83
Study Link 4·2
base-10 blocks
slate

**Key Concepts and Skills**
• Model decimals through hundredths with base-10 blocks. [Number and Numeration Goal 1]
• Read and write decimals through hundredths. [Number and Numeration Goal 1]
• Rename fractions with 100 in the denominator as decimals. [Number and Numeration Goal 5]
• Compare and order decimals through hundredths. [Number and Numeration Goal 6]

**Key Vocabulary** decimal

✔ **Ongoing Assessment:** Informing Instruction See page 251.

✔ **Ongoing Assessment:** Recognizing Student Achievement Use journal page 83.
[Number and Numeration Goal 6]

### 2 Ongoing Learning & Practice | materials

Students play *Product Pile-Up* to practice multiplication facts.

Students practice and maintain skills through Math Boxes and Study Link activities.

☐ *Math Journal 1*, p. 84
☐ *Student Reference Book*, p. 259
☐ Study Link Master (*Math Masters*, p. 112)
☐ number cards 1–10 (8 of each)

### 3 Differentiation Options | materials

**READINESS**
Students play *Coin Top-It* to practice comparing decimals in a money context.

**ENRICHMENT**
Students create riddles and order decimals to solve them.

**EXTRA PRACTICE**
Students solve problems involving decimals.

**ELL SUPPORT**
Students create a Decimals All Around Museum.

☐ Game Masters (*Math Masters*, pp. 467 and 506)
☐ scissors; coins
☐ *5-Minute Math*, pp. 14, 89, and 94
☐ *The Everything Kids' Joke Book: Side-Splitting, Rib-Tickling Fun*
☐ *Kids' Funniest Jokes*

**See Advance Preparation**

### Additional Information

**Advance Preparation** For the optional Enrichment activity in Part 3, obtain the books *The Everything Kids' Joke Book: Side-Splitting, Rib-Tickling Fun* by Michael Dahl (Adams Media Corporation, 1992) and *Kids' Funniest Jokes* edited by Shelia Anne Barry (Sterling Publishing Co., 1993).

> **Technology**
> **Assessment Management System**
> Journal page 83, Problem 1
> See the **iTLG.**

**Key Concepts and Skills** are identified for each lesson and are linked to Grade-Level Goals. They highlight the variety of mathematics that children may access in the lesson and show that each lesson has significant mathematics content for every child.

**Grade-Level Goals** are mathematical goals organized by content strand and articulated across grade levels. These goals define a progression of concepts and skills from Kindergarten through Grade 6.

**Key Vocabulary** consists of words that are new or unfamiliar to children and is consistently highlighted. Children, including English language learners, are encouraged to use this vocabulary in meaningful ways throughout the lesson in order to develop a command of mathematical language.

**Mental Math and Reflexes** problems range in difficulty, beginning with easier exercises and progressing to more-difficult ones; levels are designated by the symbols ●○○, ●●○, and ●●●. Many of these activities are presented in a "slate, chalk, and eraser" format that engages all children in answering questions and allows the teacher to quickly assess children's understanding.

**Math Messages** activate and build on children's prior knowledge and create a context for the material to be learned.

**Informing Instruction** notes suggest how to use observations of children's work to adapt instruction. These notes are designed to help the teacher anticipate and recognize common errors and misconceptions in children's thinking or to alert the teacher to multiple solution strategies or unique insights children may offer.

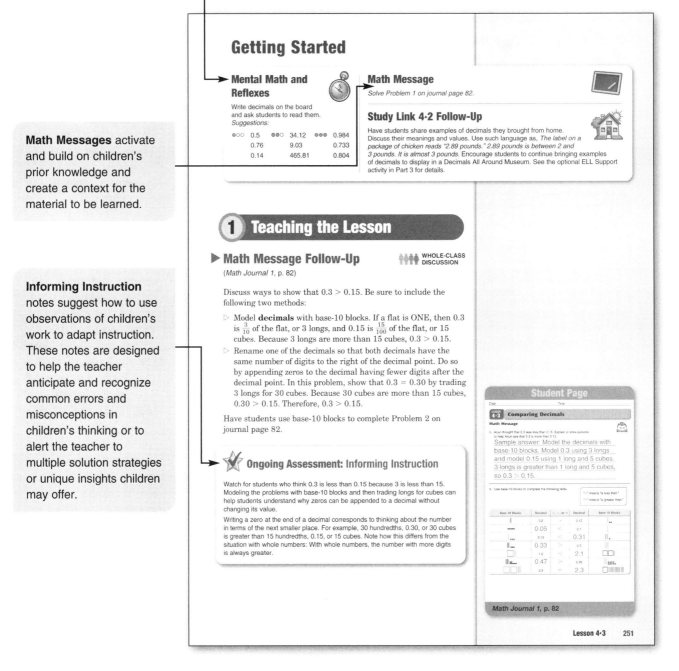

## Getting Started

### Mental Math and Reflexes

Write decimals on the board and ask students to read them. *Suggestions:*

| ●○○ | 0.5 | ●●○ | 34.12 | ●●● | 0.984 |
| | 0.76 | | 9.03 | | 0.733 |
| | 0.14 | | 465.81 | | 0.804 |

### Math Message

*Solve Problem 1 on journal page 82.*

### Study Link 4·2 Follow-Up

Have students share examples of decimals they brought from home. Discuss their meanings and values. Use such language as, *The label on a package of chicken reads "2.89 pounds." 2.89 pounds is between 2 and 3 pounds. It is almost 3 pounds.* Encourage students to continue bringing examples of decimals to display in a Decimals All Around Museum. See the optional ELL Support activity in Part 3 for details.

## 1 Teaching the Lesson

### ▶ Math Message Follow-Up
**WHOLE-CLASS DISCUSSION**

(*Math Journal 1*, p. 82)

Discuss ways to show that 0.3 > 0.15. Be sure to include the following two methods:

▷ Model **decimals** with base-10 blocks. If a flat is ONE, then 0.3 is $\frac{3}{10}$ of the flat, or 3 longs, and 0.15 is $\frac{15}{100}$ of the flat, or 15 cubes. Because 3 longs are more than 15 cubes, 0.3 > 0.15.

▷ Rename one of the decimals so that both decimals have the same number of digits to the right of the decimal point. Do so by appending zeros to the decimal having fewer digits after the decimal point. In this problem, show that 0.3 = 0.30 by trading 3 longs for 30 cubes. Because 30 cubes are more than 15 cubes, 0.30 > 0.15. Therefore, 0.3 > 0.15.

Have students use base-10 blocks to complete Problem 2 on journal page 82.

### ⭐ Ongoing Assessment: Informing Instruction

Watch for students who think 0.3 is less than 0.15 because 3 is less than 15. Modeling the problems with base-10 blocks and then trading longs for cubes can help students understand why zeros can be appended to a decimal without changing its value.

Writing a zero at the end of a decimal corresponds to thinking about the number in terms of the next smaller place. For example, 30 hundredths, 0.30, or 30 cubes is greater than 15 hundredths, 0.15, or 15 cubes. Note how this differs from the situation with whole numbers: With whole numbers, the number with more digits is always greater.

**Student Page**

Date                    Time

**4·3 Comparing Decimals**

**Math Message**

1. Arun thought that 0.3 was less than 0.15. Explain or draw pictures to help Arun see that 0.3 is more than 0.15.
Sample answer: Model the decimals with base-10 blocks. Model 0.3 using 3 longs and model 0.15 using 1 long and 5 cubes. 3 longs is greater than 1 long and 5 cubes, so 0.3 > 0.15.

2. Use base-10 blocks to complete the following table.

"<" means "is less than"
">" means "is greater than"

| Base-10 Blocks | Decimal | <, >, or = | Decimal | Base-10 Blocks |
| --- | --- | --- | --- | --- |
| | 0.2 | > | 0.12 | |
| | 0.05 | < | 0.1 | |
| | 0.13 | < | 0.31 | |
| | 0.33 | > | 0.3 | |
| | 1.2 | < | 2.1 | |
| | 0.47 | > | 0.39 | |
| | 2.3 | = | 2.3 | |

*Math Journal 1, p. 82*

Lesson 4·3      251

**Recognizing Student Achievement** notes highlight specific tasks that can be used for assessment to monitor children's progress toward Grade-Level Goals. The notes identify the expectations for a child who is making adequate progress and point to skills or strategies that some children may be able to demonstrate.

**Games** played in the classroom, online, and at home provide significant practice in *Everyday Mathematics*. Games are ideal for differentiating instruction as rules and levels of difficulty can be modified easily.

**Adjusting the Activity** notes include recommendations for tools, visual aids, and other instructional strategies that provide immediate support for exceptional learners. These notes also provide suggestions for open-ended questions to extend children's thinking. Notes labeled "ELL" include suggestions for meeting the needs of English language learners.

**Math Boxes** are designed to provide distributed practice. Math Boxes routinely revisit recent content to help children build and maintain important concepts and skills. One or two problems on each journal page preview content for the coming unit. Use class performance on these problems as you plan for the coming unit.

**Writing/Reasoning** prompts are linked to Math Boxes problems. These prompts provide children with opportunities to respond to questions that extend and deepen their mathematical thinking. In addition, these prompts offer regular opportunities for children to communicate their understanding of concepts and skills and their strategies for solving problems.

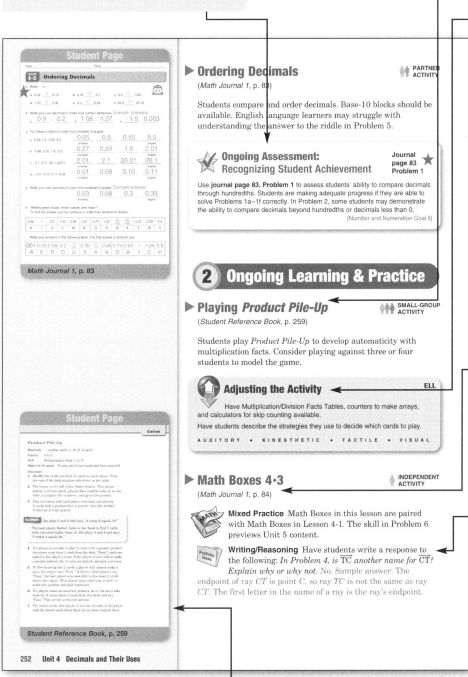

The *Student Reference Book* is a resource for children to use with their teachers, families, and classmates. It includes examples of completed problems similar to those children encounter in class, explanations, illustrations, and game directions. The *Student Reference Book* provides excellent support for all children, including English language learners and their families. At Grades 1 and 2, this book is called *My Reference Book.*

**Study Links** are the *Everyday Mathematics* version of homework assignments. At Grades 1 through 3, they are called **Home Links.** They can be assigned to promote mathematical discussions at home.

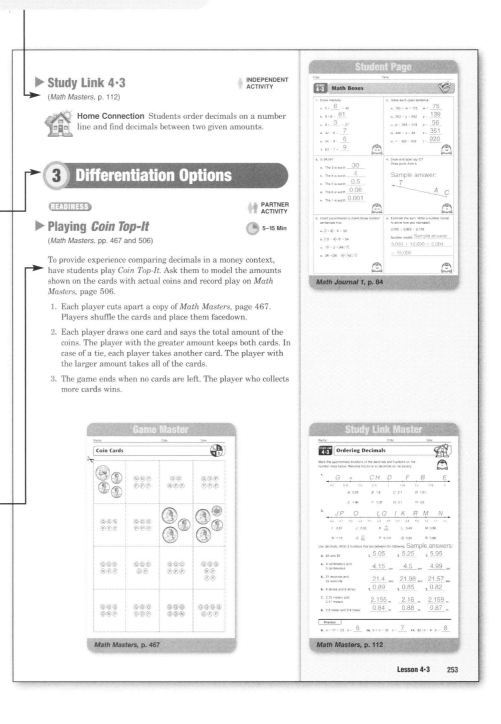

▶ **Study Link 4·3**

(*Math Masters*, p. 112)

INDEPENDENT ACTIVITY

**Home Connection** Students order decimals on a number line and find decimals between two given amounts.

### 3 Differentiation Options

**Differentiation Options** include optional Readiness, Enrichment, Extra Practice, and ELL Support activities that can be used with individual children, small groups, or the whole class. The activities build on the Key Concepts and Skills highlighted in Part 1 of each lesson. Use them to supplement, modify, or adapt the lesson to meet children's needs.

**READINESS**

PARTNER ACTIVITY

▶ **Playing *Coin Top-It***

5–15 Min

(*Math Masters*, pp. 467 and 506)

To provide experience comparing decimals in a money context, have students play *Coin Top-It*. Ask them to model the amounts shown on the cards with actual coins and record play on *Math Masters*, page 506.

1. Each player cuts apart a copy of *Math Masters*, page 467. Players shuffle the cards and place them facedown.

2. Each player draws one card and says the total amount of the coins. The player with the greater amount keeps both cards. In case of a tie, each player takes another card. The player with the larger amount takes all of the cards.

3. The game ends when no cards are left. The player who collects more cards wins.

**Readiness Activities** preview lesson content or provide children with alternative strategies for learning concepts and skills.

**Enrichment Activities** apply or deepen children's understanding of lesson content.

ENRICHMENT

PARTNER ACTIVITY

15–30 Min

### ▶ Writing Decimal Riddles

Portfolio Ideas

Literature Link To apply students' understanding of decimal concepts, have them write and solve decimal riddles similar to the one on journal page 83. The following books are good sources for riddles:

- ***The Everything Kids' Joke Book: Side-Splitting, Rib-Tickling Fun*** (Everything Kids Series) by Michael Dahl (Adams Media Corporation, 1992)
- ***Kids' Funniest Jokes,*** edited by Sheila Anne Barry (Sterling Publishing Co., 1993)

EXTRA PRACTICE

SMALL-GROUP ACTIVITY

5–15 Min

### ▶ *5-Minute Math*

To offer students more experience with decimals, see *5-Minute Math,* pages 14, 89, and 94.

ELL SUPPORT

SMALL-GROUP ACTIVITY

15–30 Min

### ▶ Creating a Decimals All Around Museum

*(Differentiation Handbook)*

To provide language support for decimals, have students create a Decimals All Around Museum. See the *Differentiation Handbook* for additional information.

Ask students to read the numbers and describe some of the ways that decimals are used in the museum; for example, what the numbers mean, the different categories of uses, or the units attached to the decimals.

254 Unit 4 Decimals and Their Uses

**Cross-Curricular Links** engage diverse groups of learners by connecting mathematics to other subject areas and to children's prior knowledge.

**Extra Practice Activities** provide children with additional practice for lesson content. For example, the activities in *5-Minute Math* for Grades 4 through 6 and in *Minute Math*®+ for Grades 1 through 3 are ideal for this purpose.

**ELL Support Activities** provide support for language development for all children, especially English language learners.

# Features for Differentiating in *Everyday Mathematics*

## General Differentiation Strategies

> *All tasks should respect each learner. Every student deserves work that is focused on the essential knowledge, understanding, and skills targeted for the lesson. Every student should be required to think at a high level and should find his or her work interesting and powerful.*
>
> (Tomlinson 2003, 61, 2: 9)

Each *Everyday Mathematics* lesson focuses on a range of mathematical concepts and skills. The most prominent of these are highlighted in the *Key Concepts and Skills* section at the beginning of the lesson. Planning for differentiated instruction involves analyzing which Key Concepts and Skills are appropriate as learning objectives for individual children and then supporting, emphasizing, and enhancing these concepts and skills when teaching the lesson.

Examples of some of the instructional strategies incorporated into *Everyday Mathematics* lessons are described here. These strategies will help you support, emphasize, and enhance lesson content to ensure that all children, including English language learners, are engaged in the mathematics at their appropriate developmental level.

### Framing the Lesson

Lesson introductions set the stage and support learning by mentally preparing children for the content of the lesson or by activating prior knowledge. For example, you might begin a geometry lesson with one of the following:

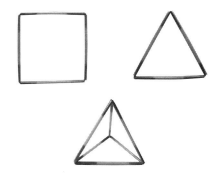

◆ Remind children that they were working on 2-dimensional shapes in the last lesson. Have them discuss what they remember about 2-dimensional shapes.

◆ Tell children that today they are going to build geometric shapes using straws. Ask: *What are some things you know about shapes that will help you with this activity?*

## Providing Wait Time

Lessons consist of whole-class, small-group, partner, and independent work. During the whole-class portion of a lesson, allow time for children to think and process information before eliciting answers to questions posed. Waiting even a few seconds for an answer will help many children process information and, in turn, participate more fully in class discussions.

Wait time is also beneficial when you pose Mental Math and Reflexes problems. Encourage children to stop and think before they write on their slates and show their answers. Consider displaying the three steps on a poster. Establish a routine by pointing to the steps in sequence, pausing at each for several seconds.

*Establish a routine using Mental Math and Reflexes in which children* Think, Write, *and* Show.

## Making Connections to Everyday Life

Lessons offer regular opportunities to build on children's everyday life by helping them make connections between their everyday experiences and new mathematics concepts and skills.

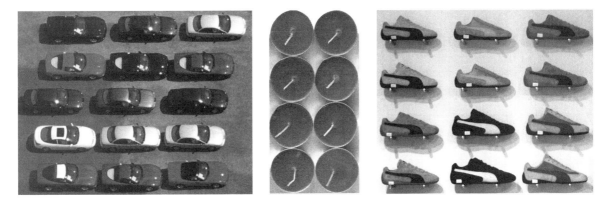

*Children build an Array Museum to display examples of arrays found in everyday life. Arrays are closely related to equal-groups situations. If the equal groups are arranged in rows and columns, then a rectangular array is formed. As with equal-group situations, arrays can lead to either multiplication or division problems.*

## Modeling Concretely

*Everyday Mathematics* lessons frequently include the use of manipulatives. Make them easily available at all times and for all children. Modeling concretely not only makes lesson content more accessible for some children, but it can also deepen all children's understanding of concepts and skills.

◆ Have counters available so children can model number stories.

*Julie had 3 apples and Marcus had 4 apples.*
*How many apples did they have in all?*

◆ Have coins available so children can model coin combinations or problems that involve making change.

*Show 35¢ in two different ways.*

◆ Have base-10 blocks available so children can model place value, addition, and subtraction.

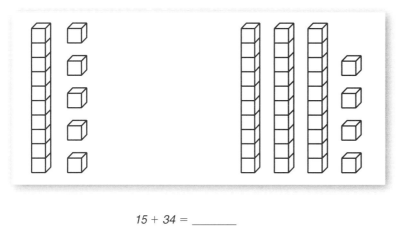

*15 + 34 = _____*

## Modeling Visually

Classrooms tend to be highly verbal places, and this can be overwhelming for some children. Simple chalkboard drawings, diagrams, and other visual representations can help children make sense of the flow of words around them and can also help them connect words to the actual items.

◆ Use pictures to model even and odd numbers.

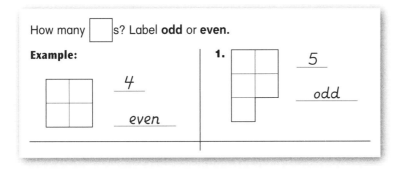

◆ Use arrays to model square numbers.

Complete the facts.

1. $1 \times 1 = \underline{1}$
2. $2 \times 2 = \underline{4}$
3. $3 \times 3 = \underline{9}$
4. $4 \times 4 = \underline{16}$
5. $5 \times 5 = \underline{25}$
6. $6 \times 6 = \underline{36}$
7. $7 \times 7 = \underline{49}$
8. $8 \times 8 = \underline{64}$
9. $9 \times 9 = \underline{81}$
10. $10 \times 10 = \underline{100}$

◆ Use a number line to visually model division by a fraction.

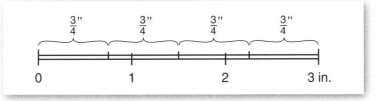

*To illustrate division of a whole number by a fraction, children partition a 3-inch segment into equal $\frac{3}{4}$-inch segments. Children ask the question, "How many $\frac{3}{4}$-inch segments are in 3 inches?" They answer the question by counting the number of line segments; in this case, there are 4 equal segments. Children then write the number sentence, $3 \div \frac{3}{4} = 4$.*

## Modeling Physically

Lessons suggest ways to have children demonstrate concepts and skills with gestures or movements. This strategy helps many children better understand and retain the concept or skill.

◆ Have children model the concept of *parallel* by holding their arms in front of them, parallel to each other.

*A physical model for parallel line segments*

◆ Have children model addition and subtraction problems by moving their fingers on number lines or number grids. A number-grid master can be found on page 132 of this handbook.

| –9 | –8 | –7 | –6 | –5 | –4 | –3 | –2 | –1 | 0 |
|---|---|---|---|---|---|---|---|---|---|
| 1 | 2 | 3 | 4 | 5 | 6 | 7 | 8 | 9 | 10 |
| 11 | 12 | 13 | 14 | 15 | 16 | 17 | 18 | 19 | 20 |
| 21 | 22 | 23 | 24 | 25 | 26 | 27 | 28 | 29 | 30 |
| 31 | 32 | 33 | 34 | 35 | 36 | 37 | 38 | 39 | 40 |
| 41 | 42 | 43 | 44 | 45 | 46 | 47 | 48 | 49 | 50 |
| 51 | 52 | 53 | 54 | 55 | 56 | 57 | 58 | 59 | 60 |
| 61 | 62 | 63 | 64 | 65 | 66 | 67 | 68 | 69 | 70 |
| 71 | 72 | 73 | 74 | 75 | 76 | 77 | 78 | 79 | 80 |
| 81 | 82 | 83 | 84 | 85 | 86 | 87 | 88 | 89 | 90 |
| 91 | 92 | 93 | 94 | 95 | 96 | 97 | 98 | 99 | 100 |
| 101 | 102 | 103 | 104 | 105 | 106 | 107 | 108 | 109 | 110 |

*15 + 33 = _____*

◆ Have children skip count on a calculator while doing a class count. This strategy reinforces counting visually by showing the numbers while at the same time physically engaging children.

*Program a TI-108 calculator to count by 2s. Clear the calculator. Enter 2 ⊞ ⊟ and repeatedly enter ⊟ without clearing the calculator.*

## Providing Organizational Tools

Lessons provide a variety of tools to help children organize their thinking. Have children use diagrams, tables, charts, and graphs when these materials are included in lessons and as appropriate. This is another way to make the lesson content more accessible for some children while at the same time deepening other children's understanding of concepts and skills.

◆ Have children use Venn diagrams to compare and contrast properties of numbers, shapes, and so on.

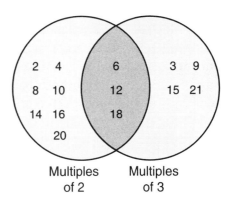

*Blank masters for Venn diagrams can be found on pages 133 and 134 of this handbook.*

◆ Have children use situation diagrams to model operations. Blank masters for these diagrams can be found on pages 135 and 136 of this handbook.

| rows | chairs per row | chairs in all |
|------|----------------|---------------|
| 3 | ? | 15 |

*Adriana set up chairs in her backyard for a play. She had 15 chairs in all. She made 3 rows. How many chairs were in each row?*

| Total ? | |
|---------|---------|
| **Part** 47 | **Part** 15 |

*Malcolm had 47 pennies in a jar in his room. His brother had 15 pennies. How many pennies did they have in all?*

◆ Provide children with place-value charts or have them draw their own. Have them write numbers in the charts as dictated, for example, the number that has a 3 in the thousands place, a 2 in the ones place, a 4 in the ten-thousands place, and a 0 everywhere else.

| Ten Thousands | Thousands | Hundreds | Tens | Ones |
|---------------|-----------|----------|------|------|
| 4 | 3 | 0 | 0 | 2 |

## Engaging Children in Talking about Math

Lessons often suggest discussion prompts or questions that support the development of good communication skills in the context of mathematics. Although finding the correct solution is one important goal, *Everyday Mathematics* lessons also emphasize sharing and comparing solution strategies. This type of "math talk" involves not only explaining what is done (explanation), but also why it is done (reasoning), and why it is correct or incorrect to do it a particular way (justification). These discussions help children deepen their understanding of mathematical concepts and processes. Encourage children to look at other children when they are speaking. You may want to model the difference between hearing and listening to help children understand what is expected of them.

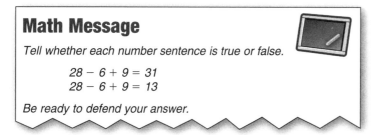

**Math Message**

*Tell whether each number sentence is true or false.*

$$28 - 6 + 9 = 31$$
$$28 - 6 + 9 = 13$$

*Be ready to defend your answer.*

*Some children may work the problems from left to right and determine that the first number sentence is true. Other children may decide that the second number sentence is true by first adding 6 and 9 and then subtracting the sum from 28. Others may reason that both sentences could be true, depending on what you do first. This Math Message problem and the resulting discussion serve as an introduction to the use of parentheses in number sentences that involve more than one operation.*

## Engaging Children in Writing about Math

Journal pages and assessment problems frequently prompt children to explain their thinking and strategies in words, pictures, and diagrams. Writing offers children opportunities to reflect on their thinking and can help you assess their mathematical understandings and communication skills. Exit Slips and Math Logs are ideal places for children to record their thinking.

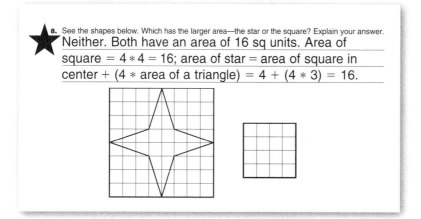

**8.** See the shapes below. Which has the larger area—the star or the square? Explain your answer.

Neither. Both have an area of 16 sq units. Area of square $= 4 * 4 = 16$; area of star $=$ area of square in center $+ (4 * $ area of a triangle$) = 4 + (4 * 3) = 16.$

*Children demonstrate their understanding of area by responding to the question on the journal page.*

## Using Key Concepts and Skills

Each *Everyday Mathematics* lesson provides children with opportunities to explore a variety of mathematics. This variety allows you to target appropriate concepts and skills for individual children.

Shown below are the Key Concepts and Skills in Lesson 3-4 of *Third Grade Everyday Mathematics*.

**Key Concepts and Skills**
- Use basic facts to find perimeter. [Operations and Computation Goal 1]
- Model polygons with straws; identify and describe polygons. [Geometry Goal 2]
- Measure sides of polygons to the nearest inch. [Measurement and Reference Frames Goal 1]
- Add side lengths to find perimeter. [Measurement and Reference Frames Goal 2]

At the beginning of the lesson, children use straws and connectors to build the polygons in Problems 1 and 2 on journal page 63 and compare the properties of these polygons. Children then work on the journal page.

◆ Modeling and describing polygons and measuring the lengths of the sides may be reasonable skills to target for some children in this lesson. These children might complete only Problems 1 and 2 on journal page 63.

◆ Problems 1 and 2 may be the most important ones for some children to complete. Encourage children to complete these problems first and to finish the remainder of the page if they have time, comparing their answers with one another. Circulate and assist.

◆ Finding perimeters may be a reasonable skill to emphasize for some children. If children completed Problem 4 by drawing a rectangle with a perimeter of 20, ask them to apply their understanding of perimeter by drawing other rectangles on a grid with perimeters of 20. Have children write an explanation of how they can be sure they found all such rectangles.

◆ Some children may need more time to complete all the problems. Have children who do not complete the page during the course of the lesson complete it later as time and experience allow.

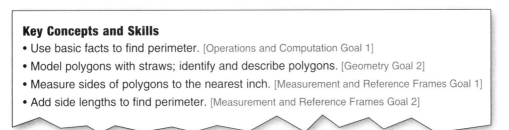

Math Journal 1, *page 63, reflects the Key Concepts and Skills in Lesson 3-4 of* Third Grade Everyday Mathematics.

## Summarizing the Lesson

Lesson summaries offer children a chance to bring closure to the lesson, reflect on the concepts and skills they have learned, and pose questions they may still have about the lesson content. Exit Slips and Math Logs are ideal places for children to record their reflections about what they learned. For example, a lesson on measurement might close with one of the following:

◆ Have children describe what they learned about standard units of linear measure.

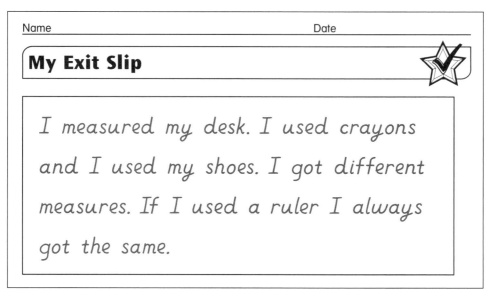

| Name | Date |
|---|---|

**My Exit Slip**

I measured my desk. I used crayons and I used my shoes. I got different measures. If I used a ruler I always got the same.

*Using an Exit Slip, a child describes what she learned.*

◆ Have children record what they know about using a ruler to measure length.

**My Exit Slip**

When I use a ruler to measure length I have to line up one edge of the line segment with the 0 on the ruler. Sometimes the 0 isn't at the edge.

*Using an Exit Slip, a child explains how he uses a ruler.*

# Vocabulary Development

*It is of interest to note that while some dolphins are reported to have learned English—up to fifty words in correct context—no human being has been reported to have learned dolphinese.*

—Carl Sagan
(Robertson 1998, 364)

The most effective way for children, including English language learners, to learn new words is to encounter them repeatedly in meaningful contexts. When the meaning of a new word is understood, real mastery requires using it in conversation and writing. With this principle in mind, *Everyday Mathematics* incorporates many opportunities within the lessons for children to develop vocabulary. *For example:*

◆ Topics and concepts are regularly revisited throughout the program, so children are constantly building on and deepening their understanding of mathematical terms from previous lessons.

◆ Hands-on, interactive, and visual activities in each lesson ensure that new words are introduced in clear, comprehensible ways.

◆ Sharing solutions and explanations, along with cooperative group work, ensures that children have opportunities to use new vocabulary purposefully.

Examples of helpful strategies are described here.

## Providing Visual References

Suggest visual references to provide support for the use and development of mathematical language.

◆ Have children underline the names of the pattern blocks with a pencil that is the same color as the corresponding block to help children associate the words with the shapes.

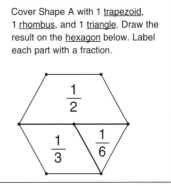

Cover Shape A with 1 <u>trapezoid</u>, 1 <u>rhombus</u>, and 1 <u>triangle</u>. Draw the result on the <u>hexagon</u> below. Label each part with a fraction.

◆ Record the words and the number model for a number story.

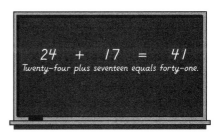

## Using *My Reference Book*

*My Reference Book* is a rich resource for definitions and examples of vocabulary. Teach children how to use the table of contents and the index to make optimal use of this resource. *My Reference Book* is also a good source of illustrations that English language learners often find useful.

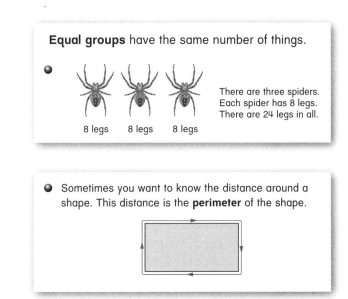

**Creating a Language-Rich Environment**

Support children's development of their mathematics vocabulary by immersing them in a language-rich environment. Seeing, hearing, and using new terms in meaningful ways will help them navigate through the language-rich mathematics lessons and will support their development of stronger communication skills.

◆ Display new vocabulary on a Math Word Wall. Include illustrations so that children can make sense of the words and use them in their speech and writing.

◆ Use mathematical terminology whenever possible during class discussions. For example, instead of saying, *A square has four corners,* say something like, *A square has four vertices, or corners.*

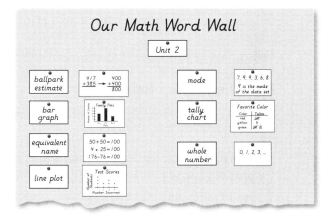

*Samples from a Math Word Wall*

◆ Post labels in the classroom that will help children connect their everyday lives to the mathematics they are studying.

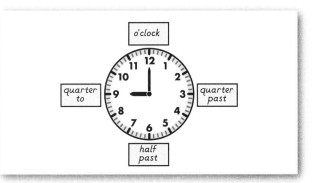

*Label your classroom clock.*

## Recording Key Ideas

On the board or Class Data Pad, record in words, symbols, and pictures the key ideas or key solution steps that children share during class discussions. *For example:*

During a class discussion, one child shares the following strategy when explaining how he solved 31 – 14. "First I took 10 from the 14 and subtracted it from 30 because there is a 30 and a 1 in 31. I had 21 left. Then I counted back 4 more for the 4 I had left from 14. I started with 21, then counted, 20, 19, 18, 17. I was holding up four fingers, so I knew I counted back 4."

*Record the steps of a child's strategy on the board.*

## Clarifying the Meaning of Words

Lessons routinely highlight potentially confusing words and provide suggestions for clarifying their meanings. Such words include those with multiple meanings, such as *power,* and homophones (words that are pronounced the same, but differ in meaning), such as *sum* and *some.*

◆ Discuss the everyday versus the mathematical usage of the word *change.*

◆ Discuss the different meanings of the word *power* in the terms *fact power* and *power of a number.*

◆ Write *some* and *sum* on the board. Discuss and clarify the meaning of each word.

*Illustrate the difference between* sum *and* some.

# Games

Frequent practice is necessary for children to build and maintain strong mental-arithmetic skills and reflexes. There are many opportunities in *Everyday Mathematics* for practice through games. Games are not merely attractive add-ons but an essential component of the *Everyday Mathematics* program and curriculum.

*Everyday Mathematics* games are important for these reasons:

◆ Games help children develop the ability to think critically and solve problems. The variety of games in *Everyday Mathematics* lays the foundation for increasingly difficult concepts and helps children develop sophisticated solution strategies.

◆ Games provide an effective and interactive way for children to practice and master basic concepts and skills. Practice through playing games not only builds fact and operation skills, but often reinforces other concepts and skills, such as calculator use, money exchange, geometric intuition, and ideas about probability.

◆ Games have advantages over paper-and-pencil drills.

| Games | Paper-and-Pencil Drills |
|---|---|
| Present enjoyable ways to practice skills | Tend toward tedium and monotony |
| Can be played during free time, lunch and recess, or even at home | Are used only during required class time |
| Are worksheet-free | Are worksheet-based |
| Are easily adaptable for a class of children who need to practice a wide range of skills at a variety of levels | Require a variety of worksheets to practice different skills at a variety of levels |
| Provide immediate insight into children's understanding through their discussions and conversations about mathematics | Result in attempts to understand children's thinking while grading worksheets that are days old |

Spend some time learning the *Everyday Mathematics* games so that you understand how much they contribute to children's mathematical progress and can join in the fun.

## Using Games in the Classroom

Games can be used in many ways. Consider these ideas for making games both enjoyable and educational for all children:

◆ Establish a routine to provide all children the opportunity to play games at least two or three times each week for a total of about one hour per week. Practice is most effective when it is distributed, so several short practice sessions are preferable to one large block of time.

◆ Establish a routine for playing games as a regular part of your math class rather than as a reward for completing assigned work. It is important that all children have time to play games, especially children who work at a slower pace or who may need more practice than their classmates do. This way, children who need the practice the most will not miss out.

◆ Set up a Games Corner with some of the children's favorite games. Be sure to include all of the gameboards, materials, and game record sheets needed. Consider creating a task card for each game. Encourage children to visit this corner during free time. Change the games menu frequently to correspond with concepts currently taught in your classroom and to offer children additional practice and review of particular skills.

> BEAT THE CALCULATOR
> See My Reference Book
> pages 124 and 125 for rules.
>
> Materials you need:
> number cards 0–9 (4 of each)
> calculator

*Sample task card for* Beat the Calculator

◆ Establish game stations where children can rotate to a new station about every 15 minutes. Station time can occur at the beginning or the end of a lesson, during the entire mathematics time, or when a substitute teacher is in the classroom. Consider asking parent volunteers to assist at stations. Provide parents with game directions ahead of time so they are familiar with the rules and with the concepts or skills practiced.

◆ Monitor children when they play games. Ask children to explain the concept or skill they are practicing or describe strategies they are using.

◆ Consider children's strengths carefully when pairing or grouping them. Group children so that they can support one another's learning.

- If it is a new game, consider pairing children who will readily understand and implement the rules with children who may need assistance learning the game.

- If a familiar game can be played at a variety of levels, consider pairing children who are working at the same level.

◆ Have children complete game record sheets so they are accountable for the work they do. Alternatively, have children complete Exit Slips summarizing the concepts or skills they practiced.

## *Dime-Nickel-Penny Grab* Record Sheet

| | Dimes | Nickels | Pennies | My Total | My Partner's Total |
|---|---|---|---|---|---|
| **Round 1** | Ⓓ Ⓓ Ⓓ | Ⓝ Ⓝ | Ⓟ | 41¢ | (46¢) |
| **Round 2** | Ⓓ Ⓓ | Ⓝ Ⓝ Ⓝ Ⓝ | Ⓟ Ⓟ | 47¢ | (68¢) |
| **Round 3** | | | | | |
| **Round 4** | | | | | |
| **Round 5** | | | | | |
| **Round 6** | | | | | |
| **Round 7** | | | | | |

*First-grade children complete a* Dime-Nickel-Penny Grab *record sheet. They draw* Ⓓ, Ⓝ, *and* Ⓟ *in the chart to record the coins they grabbed. Children then record their total and their partner's total. Finally, they circle the greater number of cents in each round.*

## Modifying Games

Games are easily adapted to meet a variety of practice needs. For example, you can engage all children in the same game at a variety of levels. The modification strategies suggested below can be used for most games included in *Everyday Mathematics*. For specific variations, see the game adaptations in the unit-specific section of this handbook beginning on page 49.

◆ Modify the level of difficulty of games by targeting a certain range of numbers for children working at different levels. Because numbers in most games are generated randomly, you can modify blank spinners, decrease or increase the number of dice, roll polyhedral dice, or use specific sets of number cards.

Two 6-sided dice for regular game play

Two 8-sided dice to increase the range of numbers

One 10-sided die (0 through 9) to decrease the range of numbers

◆ Modify the level of difficulty of games by encouraging children to play a mental-math version of a game in which children would normally use paper and pencil to calculate scores.

◆ See whether variations of a game are available so you can target different concepts or skills or different levels for children appropriately. Many *Everyday Mathematics* games provide a range of practice options by including a variety of gameboards or rules.

| Hitting Table | |
|---|---|
| **1 to 10 Facts** | |
| 1 to 21 | Out |
| 24 to 45 | Single (1 base) |
| 48 to 70 | Double (2 bases) |
| 72 to 81 | Triple (3 bases) |
| 90 to 100 | Home Run (4 bases) |

| Hitting Table | |
|---|---|
| **10 * 10s Game** | |
| 100 to 2,000 | Out |
| 2,100 to 4,000 | Single (1 base) |
| 4,200 to 5,400 | Double (2 bases) |
| 5,600 to 6,400 | Triple (3 bases) |
| 7,200 to 8,100 | Home Run (4 bases) |

*Versions of* Baseball Multiplication *provide practice with different levels of multiplication skills, for example, facts for 1 through 10 and extended facts.*

◆ Have slates on hand for children to draw pictures as they work through problems.

◆ Make various manipulatives, such as coins and bills, base-10 blocks, and counters available to provide concrete models for practicing concepts and skills.

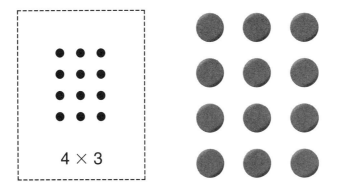

*To reinforce multiplication concepts, have children use counters to build the array shown on an* Array Bingo *card.*

◆ Introduce game-specific or mathematical vocabulary with visual cues, such as writing the terms on the board, as well as auditory support, such as having the class repeat the word aloud as a group. Use new vocabulary consistently and be careful to avoid interchanging or substituting synonymous terms, which can cause confusion for some children.

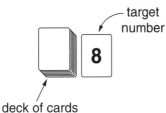

Target number *is a term frequently used in game play.*

◆ Modify the difficulty of games involving target numbers by limiting the numbers that children use. As children gain proficiency, provide larger numbers. Try this with decimals also.

*Children playing* Hit the Target *agree on a 2-digit multiple of 10 as the target number for each round. Players then select a starting number and use their calculators to add or subtract to change the starting number to the target number. You can modify the game by suggesting that children choose as the target number a multiple of 10 less than or equal to 40 or a 3- or 4-digit multiple of 100.*

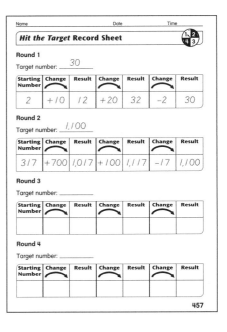

◆ Provide tools such as Addition/Subtraction or Multiplication/Division Facts Tables or calculators for children to check facts quickly and assist them in playing games that require fluency with facts they are learning.

| +, − | 0 | 1 | 2 | 3 | 4 | 5 | 6 | 7 | 8 | 9 | 10 |
|---|---|---|---|---|---|---|---|---|---|---|---|
| 0 | 0 | 1 | 2 | 3 | 4 | 5 | 6 | 7 | 8 | 9 | 10 |
| 1 | 1 | 2 | 3 | 4 | 5 | 6 | 7 | 8 | 9 | 10 | 11 |
| 2 | 2 | 3 | 4 | 5 | 6 | 7 | 8 | 9 | 10 | 11 | 12 |
| 3 | 3 | 4 | 5 | 6 | 7 | 8 | 9 | 10 | 11 | 12 | 13 |
| 4 | 4 | 5 | 6 | 7 | 8 | 9 | 10 | 11 | 12 | 13 | 14 |
| 5 | 5 | 6 | 7 | 8 | 9 | 10 | 11 | 12 | 13 | 14 | 15 |
| 6 | 6 | 7 | 8 | 9 | 10 | 11 | 12 | 13 | 14 | 15 | 16 |
| 7 | 7 | 8 | 9 | 10 | 11 | 12 | 13 | 14 | 15 | 16 | 17 |
| 8 | 8 | 9 | 10 | 11 | 12 | 13 | 14 | 15 | 16 | 17 | 18 |
| 9 | 9 | 10 | 11 | 12 | 13 | 14 | 15 | 16 | 17 | 18 | 19 |
| 10 | 10 | 11 | 12 | 13 | 14 | 15 | 16 | 17 | 18 | 19 | 20 |

*Addition/Subtraction Facts Table*

◆ Use illustrations to depict game directions. Create illustrations before introducing the game or during class discussion while introducing the game. Alternatively, have children create the illustrations after they have played the game. Children can refer to the illustrated instructions each time the game is revisited.

Deal 5 cards to each player.

◆ Encourage questions and discussion during games so children can use new vocabulary.

**Number Top-It Mat (7-Digit)**

| | Millions | Hundred Thousands | Ten Thousands | Thousands | Hundreds | Tens | Ones |
|---|---|---|---|---|---|---|---|
| **Andy** | 7 | 6 | 4 | 5 | 2 | 0 | 1 |
| **Barb** | 4 | 9 | 7 | 3 | 5 | 2 | 4 |

*Children playing* Number Top-It *use randomly generated digits to build the largest number possible. Encourage children to discuss and compare strategies for deciding where to place the digits.*

# Math Boxes

In *Everyday Mathematics,* Math Boxes are one of the main components for reviewing and maintaining skills. Math Boxes are not intended to reinforce the content of the lesson in which they appear. Rather, they provide continuous distributed practice of concepts and skills targeted in the Grade-Level Goals. It is not necessary for children to complete the Math Boxes page on the same day the lesson is taught, but it is important that the problems for each lesson are completed.

Several features of Math Boxes pages make them useful for differentiating instruction:

◆ Math Boxes in most lessons are linked with Math Boxes in one or two other lessons so that they have similar problems. Because linked Math Boxes pages target the same concepts and skills, they may be useful as extra practice tools.

◆ Writing/Reasoning prompts in the *Teacher's Lesson Guide* provide children with opportunities to respond to questions that extend and deepen their mathematical thinking. Using these prompts, children communicate their understanding of concepts and skills and their strategies for solving problems.

◆ Many Math Boxes problems include an icon for *My Reference Book.* This cue tells children where they can find help for completing the problems.

◆ One or two problems on each Math Boxes page preview content from the coming unit. Use these problems identified in the *Teacher's Lesson Guide* to assess children's performance and to build your differentiation plan.

◆ The multiple-choice format of some problems provides children with an opportunity to answer questions in a standardized-test format. The choices include *distractors* that represent common errors. Use the incorrect answers to identify and address children's needs.

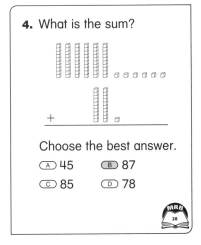

*Children choosing 78 may have reversed the digits in the sum because they do not recognize the value of the base-10 blocks.*

## Using Math Boxes in the Classroom

Math Boxes can be used in many ways. Consider these ideas for making Math Boxes a productive learning experience for all children:

◆ Create a cardstock template that allows children to focus on only one problem at a time. Or, have children use stick-on notes to cover all but one problem.

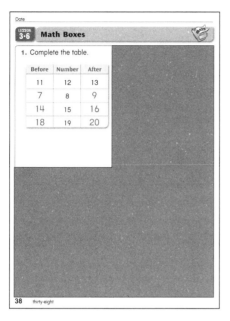 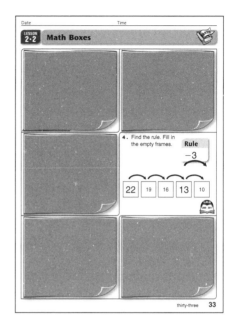

*Children can focus on one Math Boxes problem at a time.*

◆ Identify the problem or problems that are essential. Encourage children to complete these problems first. Suggest that children who finish a task early use their spare time to complete any unfinished Math Boxes problems. Consider providing time in your weekly schedule so that all children have the opportunity to complete unfinished Math Boxes problems.

◆ Have children complete the problems independently. Then have them form small groups and share their answers and explanations. As an alternative, ask children to complete the problems cooperatively even though the lesson indicates independent work.

◆ Divide the class into groups. Have each group solve one of the Math Boxes problems. "Jigsaw" to form new groups. Each of the new groups now has one child from each of the original groups. Each child in the new group is an expert on one of the problems. The expert explains the problem to the other children in the group.

◆ Have children complete Math Boxes pages as part of their daily morning routine. Math Boxes are one of the components of a lesson that lends itself to being completed outside of regular math time.

## Modifying Math Boxes

The strategies suggested here can be used for many types of Math Boxes problems. The same types of modifications can be made to other journal pages as well.

◆ Modify the range of the numbers or ask children to record measurements to a more-precise or less-precise degree of accuracy to focus on a different level of a concept or skill.

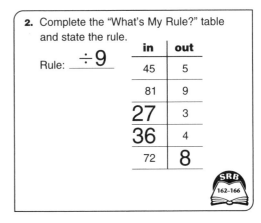

*To practice extended facts instead of basic facts, have children attach a zero to each number in the "What's My Rule?" table.*

◆ Make various manipulatives, such as coins and bills, base-10 blocks, pattern blocks, and counters, available to provide concrete models for practicing concepts and skills.

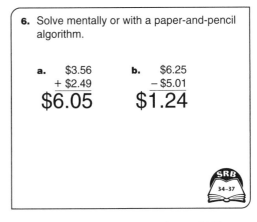

*Encourage children to use coins and bills to help them solve decimal addition and subtraction problems.*

◆ Have tools, such as number grids, place-value charts, calculators, or fact tables, available to help children solve problems.

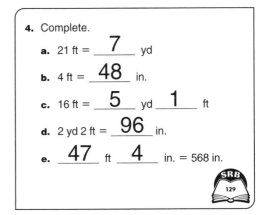

*Some children may be able to solve Problems a.–c. mentally but choose to use a calculator with Problems d. and e.*

## Creating Your Own Math Boxes

Occasionally, you may want to create your own Math Boxes page for practice or assessment purposes. There are blank masters on pages 120–125 of this handbook to serve this purpose. Consider the following ideas while designing pages for your class or individual children:

◆ Create a set of problems that focuses on a single concept or skill that children need to review, but address it in a variety of contexts. For example, focus on addition through number stories, facts problems, "What's My Rule?" problems, or skip counting. Because each Math Boxes page in the journal includes a variety of problems, each one targeting a different concept or skill, this strategy can help children who struggle with these transitions.

◆ Create a Math Boxes page that links with a set of Math Boxes pages in the journal. Tailor the numbers to meet the individual needs of children.

◆ Create a set of extra-practice problems in which all cells focus on concepts or skills from a particular lesson.

◆ Adapt *Minute Math*®+ problems that address concepts or skills children need to review.

◆ Create a page in which each problem targets a specific concept or skill. Use the page for one week, each day replacing the numbers in the problems with new numbers.

◆ Use the templates of routines found on pages 122–125 of this handbook to create Math Boxes pages for children to complete. Fill in some of the numbers for each routine. Or, have children create the Math Boxes for classmates to complete. For more information about each of these routines, see the *Teacher's Reference Manual*.™

◆ Have children write number stories in each cell of a template. Specify which operation should be the focus of each problem. Have children exchange Math Boxes pages and solve one another's problems.

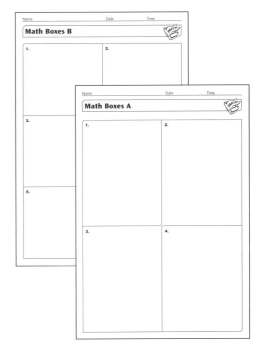

*Differentiation Masters, pages 120 and 121, are templates for blank Math Boxes pages for four or six problems.*

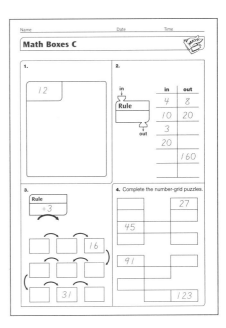

*Differentiation Masters, page 122, is a master for a blank Math Boxes page that includes a variety of routines.*

# Using Part 3 of the Lesson

As written, *Everyday Mathematics* lessons engage a wide range of learners and support the development of mathematics concepts and skills at the highest possible level. There are times, however, when teachers still need to be flexible in implementing lessons. To address the individual needs of children, Part 3 of each lesson, Differentiation Options, provides additional resources beyond the scope of what is included in Part 1. The activities suggested are optional, intended to support rather than to replace lesson content. Many of the activities, designed so children can work with partners or small groups, are ideally suited for station work. Based on your professional judgment and assessments, determine when children might benefit from these activities. For each unit, use the master found on page 138 of this handbook to plan how you will use the Part 3 activities with the whole class, small groups, or individual children.

| Lesson | Readiness | Enrichment | Extra Practice | ELL Support |
|---|---|---|---|---|
| 1-1 | | Whole class | | Carlos Andres |
| 1-2 | Abby Conner Jamal | Chantel Eric | Matt Amy | |
| 1-3 | | | Cheryl DeAndre Melissa | Melanie |
| 1-4 | Toya Takako Kevin | | Whole class | |
| 1-5 | | Isabel Leon | | Whole class |
| 1-6 | Whole class | | Whole class | |
| 1-7 | Katherine Aman | Jayne | Hannah Abby Tom | Dmitry Carlos |

**Part 3 Planning Master**

## Readiness Activities

Readiness activities introduce or develop the lesson content to support children as they work with the Key Concepts and Skills. Use Readiness activities with some or all children before teaching the lesson to preview the content so children are better prepared to engage in lesson activities. As an alternative, use Readiness activities at the completion of lesson activities to solidify children's understanding of lesson content.

In Lesson 3-1 of *Fourth Grade Everyday Mathematics,* children discuss problems in which one quantity depends on another. They illustrate this kind of relationship between pairs of numbers with a function machine and a "What's My Rule?" table. The following is the Readiness activity for the lesson.

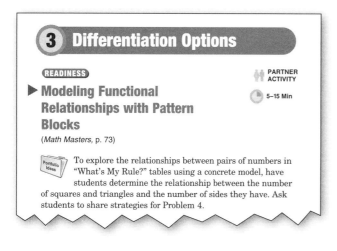

### 3 Differentiation Options

**READINESS**

**PARTNER ACTIVITY**

**5–15 Min**

▶ **Modeling Functional Relationships with Pattern Blocks**
(*Math Masters*, p. 73)

To explore the relationships between pairs of numbers in "What's My Rule?" tables using a concrete model, have students determine the relationship between the number of squares and triangles and the number of sides they have. Ask students to share strategies for Problem 4.

---

Name          Date          Time

**LESSON 3·1** "What's My Rule?" Polygon Sides

1. Use square pattern blocks to help you complete the table.

| Number of Squares | Number of Sides |
|---|---|
| 1 | 4 |
| 2 | 8 |
| 3 | 12 |
| 5 | 20 |
| 7 | 28 |
| 8 | 32 |

2. Suppose there are 12 squares. Explain how to find the number of sides without counting.
Sample answer: Multiply 12 squares by 4 sides. This equals 48 sides. (12 × 4 = 48)

3. Use triangle pattern blocks to help you complete the table.

| Number of Triangles | Number of Sides |
|---|---|
| 1 | 3 |
| 2 | 6 |
| 5 | 15 |
| 4 | 12 |
| 3 | 9 |
| 6 | 18 |

4. Suppose there are 30 sides. Explain how to find the number of triangles without counting.
Sample answer: Divide 30 sides by 3. This equals 10 triangles. (30 ÷ 3 = 10)

73

# Enrichment Activities

Enrichment activities provide ways for children to apply or further explore Key Concepts and Skills emphasized in the lesson. Use the activities with some or all children after they have completed the lesson activities.

In Lesson 8-4 of *Second Grade Everyday Mathematics,* children explore the concept of equivalent fractions by matching fractional parts of circles. The following is the Enrichment activity for the lesson.

**ENRICHMENT**

▶ **Covering Hexagons Activity**

(*Math Masters*, p. 242)

**SMALL-GROUP ACTIVITY**

5–15 Min

To apply children's understanding of equivalent fractions, have them cover hexagons with pattern blocks. Have children discuss their strategies. Children may figure out that you can split the blocks on your turn and put them in different hexagons to block and "win" hexagons. When they finish, consider having children figure out the total fraction of the board they have "won." Note: Each hexagon is $\frac{1}{7}$ of the board.

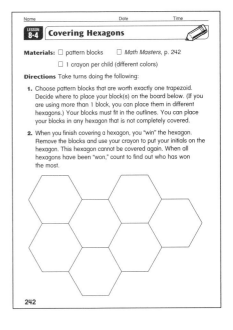

# Extra Practice Activities

These activities provide children with additional practice opportunities related to the content of the lesson. There are three main categories for extra practice activities—practice pages, games, and *Minute Math*®+ problems.

Each page of *Minute Math*®+ begins with a basic activity followed by options for adapting that activity to various ability levels. The activities not only meet the needs of your entire class or small groups of children but can also serve as catalysts for your own or children's problems and ideas.

*Minute Math*®+ activities do the following:

◆ provide reinforcement and continuous review of Grade-Level Goals;

◆ provide practice with mental arithmetic and logical thinking activities;

◆ give children additional opportunities to think and talk about mathematics and to try out new ideas by themselves or with their teachers and classmates; and

◆ promote the process of solving problems, so in the long run, children become more willing to risk sharing their thoughts and their solution strategies with classmates rather than focus on getting quick answers.

## Support for English Language Learners

The activities in the ELL Support section are designed to promote development of language related to Key Concepts and Skills. Several vocabulary routines are established early in each grade and are revisited throughout the year.

It is important to note that English language learners should not be restricted solely to ELL Support activities. Often the Readiness and Enrichment activities are ideally suited to enhance the mathematical content for this population of children. Likewise, although the activities described in this section are extremely helpful for English language learners, this kind of work enriches the vocabulary development of all children.

### Math Word Bank

Use a Math Word Bank, which is similar to a dictionary, to invite children to make connections between new terms and words and phrases they know. For each entry, have children make a visual representation of the word or phrase and list three related terms that will remind them of the meaning. Have English language learners record some of the related words in their own language. Have children keep completed pages in a 3-ring binder so that they may refer to them as necessary. Two different masters are provided for this routine on pages 126 and 127 of this handbook.

In Lesson 3-2 of *First Grade Everyday Mathematics,* children explore even and odd number patterns. The following is the ELL Support activity for this lesson.

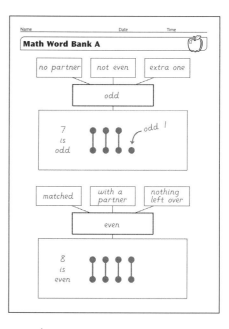

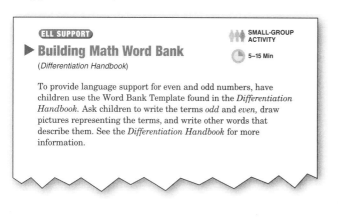

**ELL SUPPORT**

▶ **Building Math Word Bank**

(*Differentiation Handbook*)

SMALL-GROUP ACTIVITY

5–15 Min

To provide language support for even and odd numbers, have children use the Word Bank Template found in the *Differentiation Handbook.* Ask children to write the terms *odd* and *even,* draw pictures representing the terms, and write other words that describe them. See the *Differentiation Handbook* for more information.

## Museums

In *Everyday Mathematics,* museums help children connect the mathematics they are studying with their everyday lives. A museum is simply a collection of objects, pictures, or numbers that illustrates or incorporates mathematical concepts related to the lessons. Museums provide opportunities for children to explore and discuss new mathematical ideas. If several English language learners speak the same language, have them take a minute to discuss museums in their own language first and then share in English as they are able.

In Lesson 5-7 of *Second Grade Everyday Mathematics,* children construct pyramids using straws and connectors. They discuss the properties of the pyramids they have built. The following is the ELL Support activity for this lesson.

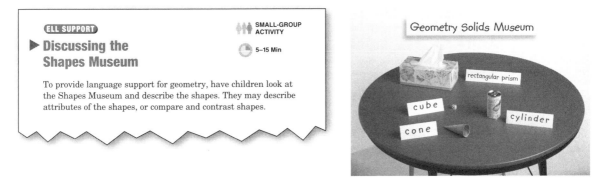

## Child- and Teacher-Made Posters

Sometimes a unit focuses on a topic that introduces potentially confusing content, for example, a great deal of new vocabulary, many steps in a problem-solving process, or several strategies for solving a problem. Providing children with a poster to use as a reference or having them create their own posters can help them make sense of such complex content.

In Unit 4 of *Fifth Grade Everyday Mathematics,* children review long-division algorithms. The following is the ELL Support activity for Lesson 4-5 in this unit.

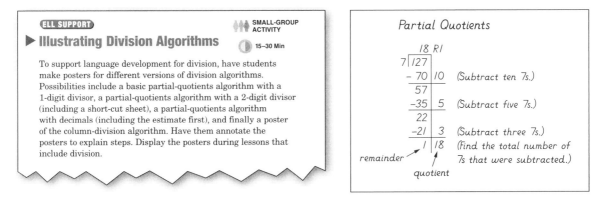

*Everyday Mathematics* also includes posters, such as the Fahrenheit Thermometer Poster. When you use the *Everyday Mathematics* posters with English language learners, you may display both the English and Spanish versions simultaneously or only the English version. Certain student pages, such as those that display various items and prices that the children use for shopping word problems, are also known as "posters."

## Graphic Organizers

Children find it easier to learn and retain new words if they connect the new words to their existing vocabulary. Graphic organizers are organizational tools for making connections more explicit and for helping children gain a deeper understanding of a concept.

In Lesson 6-10 of *Second Grade Everyday Mathematics,* children explore multiplication and division and the relationships between these operations. The following is the ELL Support activity for this lesson.

**ELL SUPPORT**

▶ **Writing Multiplication and Division Phrases**

SMALL-GROUP ACTIVITY

5–15 Min

To provide language support for understanding multiplication and division phrases, have children draw and label a table with three columns on chart paper as shown below. Ask children to identify words or phrases associated with multiplication and division. Write their responses in the table.

| Multiplication | Both Multiplication and Division | Division |
|---|---|---|
| Addition | Equal Groups | Subtraction |
| Packages of objects | Arrays | Share |
| Multiples | Fact Families | How many groups are there? |
| Skip Counting | Fact Triangles | How many in each group? |
| All Together | | Remaining |

In Lesson 8-7 of *Sixth Grade Everyday Mathematics,* children use ratios as a strategy for solving percent problems. The following is the ELL Support activity for this lesson.

**ELL SUPPORT**

▶ **Summarizing Ratio Concepts**

SMALL-GROUP ACTIVITY

5–15 Min

To provide support for language development, use a graphic organizer like the one shown below to summarize various ways to represent a ratio.

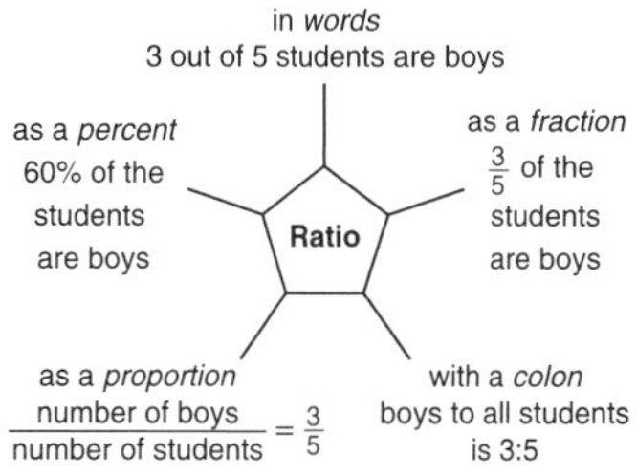

# Looking at Grade-Level Goals

Children using *Everyday Mathematics* are expected to master a great deal of mathematical content, but not necessarily the first time the concepts and skills are introduced. The *Everyday Mathematics* curriculum aims for proficiency through repeated exposure over several years of study.

All of the content in *Everyday Mathematics* is important, whether it's being treated for the first time or the fifth time. The *Everyday Mathematics* curriculum is like an intricately woven rug with many threads that appear and reappear to form complex patterns. Children will progress at different rates, so multiple exposures to important content are critical for accommodating individual differences. The program is created to be consistent with how children actually learn mathematics, building understanding over time, first through informal exposure and later through more-formal instruction. It is crucial that children have the opportunity to experience all that the curriculum has to offer in every grade.

*Everyday Mathematics* includes Grade-Level Goals, which are organized by content strand and are carefully articulated across grades. The goals define a developmentally appropriate progression of skills and concepts from Kindergarten through Grade 6. *Everyday Mathematics* is designed so that the vast majority of children will reach the Grade-Level Goals for a given grade upon completion of that grade. These Grade-Level Goals are guideposts along trajectories or paths of learning that span multiple years. Children who meet the Grade-Level Goals in *Everyday Mathematics* will be well prepared to succeed in higher levels of mathematics.

To understand where concepts and skills are revisited over time, the unit-specific section of this handbook, beginning on page 49, includes charts for looking at the Grade-Level Goals in each unit. These charts will help you see where you are in the development of the goals—whether the Grade-Level Goal is taught, practiced, or not a focus in the lessons of each unit. The excerpt below can help you understand the information these charts provide.

### Map of Number and Numeration Goal 1 for Fourth Grade

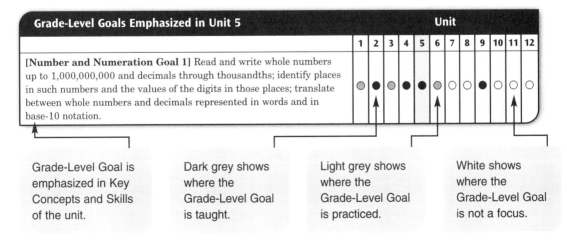

# Maintaining Concepts and Skills

The charts discussed in the previous section illustrate where each Grade-Level Goal in a unit is revisited over the course of the year. Sometimes there will be several units in a row that do not address a Grade-Level Goal through either the Key Concepts and Skills emphasized in lessons or through practice. Moreover, as the year progresses, some goals reach the end of their formal development at that grade level. Because children progress at different rates, you may sometimes have children who need to revisit concepts and skills for a particular Grade-Level Goal.

At the end of each unit overview in the unit-specific section of this handbook, you will find a list of *Maintaining Concepts and Skills* activities that you can use to provide children with additional opportunities to explore, review, or practice content. Frequently the list will include references to program routines. These routines, which are revisited throughout the curriculum across the grades, provide a comfortable and convenient way to reinforce, maintain, or further develop concepts and skills for individual children. Blank masters for these routines are included in this handbook beginning on page 119. Examples of helpful strategies are described here.

## Frames and Arrows

This routine, which is emphasized in Grades 1 through 3, provides opportunities for children to practice basic and extended addition, subtraction, and multiplication facts. The problems also require children to use algebraic thinking involving patterns, functions, and sequences.

Use these masters to create pages to meet the needs of individual children, or have children create their own problems for classmates to solve.

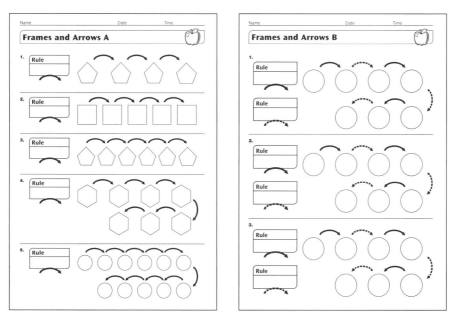

*Children use page 128, to practice solving Frames-and-Arrows problems with one rule, and page 129, to practice solving Frames-and-Arrows problems with two rules.*

## "What's My Rule?"

This routine, which is introduced in Grade 1 and continues through Grade 6, provides opportunities for children to practice basic computation skills and solve problems involving functions. In the upper grades, the functions can be represented visually in graphs and algebraically using variables. In addition to solving teacher-generated problems, children can generate problems for one another to solve. There is a blank master for "What's My Rule?" on page 130 of this handbook.

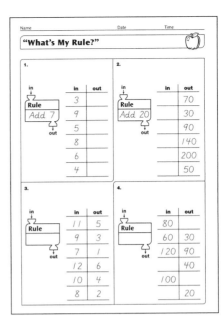

*A teacher-generated set of problems that focuses on basic and extended addition facts*

## Name-Collection Boxes

This routine, which is used in Grades 1 through 6, provides the opportunity for children to practice basic computation skills, generate equivalent names for numbers, use grouping symbols, and apply order of operations to numerical expressions. In addition to solving teacher-generated problems, children can generate problems for one another to solve. There is a blank master for name-collection boxes on page 131 of this handbook.

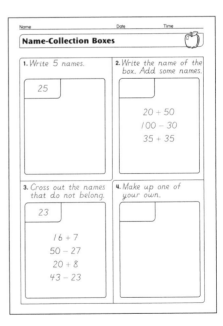

*A teacher-generated page that illustrates the variety of ways in which name-collection box problems can be formatted*

## Number Grids

This routine, which is included in Kindergarten through Grade 3, provides the opportunity for children to explore number relationships and number patterns. Children apply their understanding of these patterns and relationships when they use the number grid as a tool for solving computation problems and when they solve number-grid puzzles. When children become familiar with number-grid puzzles, the puzzles can be extended to include any range of numbers.

Name _____ Date _____ Time _____

**Number Grid**

| -9 | -8 | -7 | -6 | -5 | -4 | -3 | -2 | -1 | 0 |
|----|----|----|----|----|----|----|----|----|----|
| 1 | 2 | 3 | 4 | 5 | 6 | 7 | 8 | 9 | 10 |
| 11 | 12 | 13 | 14 | 15 | 16 | 17 | 18 | 19 | 20 |
| 21 | 22 | 23 | 24 | 25 | 26 | 27 | 28 | 29 | 30 |
| 31 | 32 | 33 | 34 | 35 | 36 | 37 | 38 | 39 | 40 |
| 41 | 42 | 43 | 44 | 45 | 46 | 47 | 48 | 49 | 50 |
| 51 | 52 | 53 | 54 | 55 | 56 | 57 | 58 | 59 | 60 |
| 61 | 62 | 63 | 64 | 65 | 66 | 67 | 68 | 69 | 70 |
| 71 | 72 | 73 | 74 | 75 | 76 | 77 | 78 | 79 | 80 |
| 81 | 82 | 83 | 84 | 85 | 86 | 87 | 88 | 89 | 90 |
| 91 | 92 | 93 | 94 | 95 | 96 | 97 | 98 | 99 | 100 |
| 101 | 102 | 103 | 104 | 105 | 106 | 107 | 108 | 109 | 110 |

- - - - - - - - - - - - - - - - - - - - - - - - - ✂ - -

| -9 | -8 | -7 | -6 | -5 | -4 | -3 | -2 | -1 | 0 |
|----|----|----|----|----|----|----|----|----|----|
| 1 | 2 | 3 | 4 | 5 | 6 | 7 | 8 | 9 | 10 |
| 11 | 12 | 13 | 14 | 15 | 16 | 17 | 18 | 19 | 20 |
| 21 | 22 | 23 | 24 | 25 | 26 | 27 | 28 | 29 | 30 |
| 31 | 32 | 33 | 34 | 35 | 36 | 37 | 38 | 39 | 40 |
| 41 | 42 | 43 | 44 | 45 | 46 | 47 | 48 | 49 | 50 |
| 51 | 52 | 53 | 54 | 55 | 56 | 57 | 58 | 59 | 60 |
| 61 | 62 | 63 | 64 | 65 | 66 | 67 | 68 | 69 | 70 |
| 71 | 72 | 73 | 74 | 75 | 76 | 77 | 78 | 79 | 80 |
| 81 | 82 | 83 | 84 | 85 | 86 | 87 | 88 | 89 | 90 |
| 91 | 92 | 93 | 94 | 95 | 96 | 97 | 98 | 99 | 100 |
| 101 | 102 | 103 | 104 | 105 | 106 | 107 | 108 | 109 | 110 |

*Differentiation Masters, page 132*

| **66** | 67 | |
|--------|-----|-----|
| | 77 | 78 |
| | **87** | |
| 96 | 97 | |
| | 107 | 108 |

*A teacher-generated number-grid puzzle that starts with 66 and 87*

| 991 | 992 | |
|------|--------|--------|
| | **1,002** | 1,003 |
| 1,011 | | 1,013 |
| 1,021 | | 1,023 |
| 1,031 | | **1,033** |

*A teacher-generated number-grid puzzle that starts with 1,002 and 1,033*

# Projects

This section offers suggestions for how to differentiate the Grade 1 Projects for your children. For each project, you will find three differentiation options: Adjusting the Activity Ideas, ELL Support, and a Writing/Reasoning prompt.

## Contents

Projects

# Geometric Gift Wrap and Greeting Cards

**Objective** To provide opportunities to use geometric shapes to create designs for gift wrap and greeting cards.

Project 1, along with all other Grade 1 projects, is located at the back of both Volume 1 and Volume 2 of the Grade 1 *Teacher's Lesson Guide*. Use this project during or after Unit 3.

## Adjusting the Activity Ideas

◆ Before children begin creating patterns, work as a group to make some sample patterns. Allow children to copy these patterns when they are producing their patterns.

◆ After children make their patterns, have them translate their shape patterns into letter patterns, for example, ABA, AABA, and so on.

◆ To make symmetrical designs with their patterns, have children make the pattern on a half-sheet of paper. Before the paint dries, have them fold the paper in half and gently press the two halves together to get the reflection of their original design across a line of symmetry.

## ELL Support

To provide language support for the Gift Wrap and Greeting Card project, gather pictures of patterns and assemble them in a *Patterns Museum*. Have children describe the patterns they see in the museum. After they have made their patterns for the gift wrap or greeting card, have children describe the patterns they have made. If several English language learners speak the same language, have them take a minute to discuss the museum in their own language first and then share what they are able to in English.

## Writing/Reasoning

Have children draw, write, or verbalize an answer to the following question: What is a pattern? A reasonable answer should explain that a pattern is something that repeats over and over again.

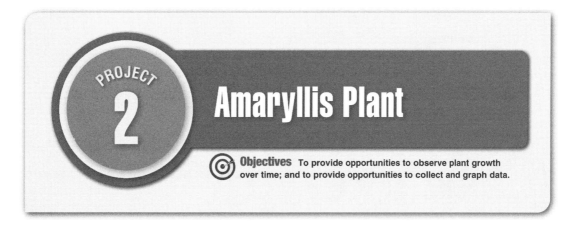

# Amaryllis Plant

**Objectives** To provide opportunities to observe plant growth over time; and to provide opportunities to collect and graph data.

Project 2, along with all other Grade 1 projects, is located at the back of both Volume 1 and Volume 2 of the Grade 1 *Teacher's Lesson Guide*. Use this project during or after Unit 4.

## Adjusting the Activity Ideas

◆ Have children measure the height of the amaryllis plant by stacking 1-inch blocks beside it. Model for children how to count the blocks from the bulb to the top of the plant.

◆ Tape a 2-foot-long strip of paper to the wall so the paper begins where the bulb begins. Have children mark the plant's growth using a crayon.

◆ Have children grow an additional amaryllis plant in the dark and compare the growth of the two plants.

## ELL Support

To provide language support for the Amaryllis Plant project, have children use the Math Word Bank template found on page 126 in this handbook. Ask children to write the term *bulb,* draw pictures representing the term, and write other related words. See page 32 of this handbook for more information.

## Writing/Reasoning

Have children draw, write, or verbalize an answer to the following question: What does the graph show about the amaryllis plant? A reasonable answer should explain that the graph shows how tall the plant was on each date.

**Objectives** To provide opportunities to estimate weight and girth; compare objects; and count a large collection of objects.

Project 3, along with all other Grade 1 projects, is located at the back of both Volume 1 and Volume 2 of the Grade 1 *Teacher's Lesson Guide*. Use this project during or after Unit 5.

## Adjusting the Activity Ideas

◆ Have children record the weights of two pumpkins, leaving a space between the numbers. Then have children compare the weights of the pumpkins using $<$, $>$, or $=$ symbols.

◆ Have children find the total number of seeds for all three pumpkins.

◆ Cut three strings to match the girth of the pumpkins. Have children match the strings to the pumpkins.

## ELL Support

To provide language support for the Pumpkin Math project, have children use the Math Word Bank template found on page 126 in this handbook. Ask children to write the term *weight,* draw a picture representing the term, and write other related words. You may want to discuss the difference between the homophones *weight* and *wait.* See page 32 of this handbook for more information.

## Writing/Reasoning

Have children draw, write, or verbalize an answer to the following question: What is girth? A reasonable answer should explain that girth is a measurement around the widest part of an object.

# All About Time

**Objective** To provide children with opportunities to explore time.

Project 4, along with all other Grade 1 projects, is located at the back of both Volume 1 and Volume 2 of the Grade 1 *Teacher's Lesson Guide*. Use this project during or after Unit 6.

## Adjusting the Activity Ideas

◆ Have children estimate how many times they could do the activities on *Math Masters,* page 300, if they had 30 seconds, 45 seconds, or 60 seconds.

◆ After making their calendars, have children determine on what day of the week their birth date will fall.

◆ Before copying *Math Masters,* page 301, fill in the name of the month and first day of each month.

## ELL Support

To provide language support for the All About Time project, have children collect pictures and objects that are used to tell and to mark off time for a *Time Museum.* The collection might include stopwatches, hourglasses, sundials, calendars, and so on. Have children discuss how the objects and pictures are similar and how they are different. If several English language learners speak the same language, have them take a minute to discuss the museum in their own language first and then share what they are able to in English.

## Writing/Reasoning

Have children draw, write, or verbalize an answer to the following question: How are calendars helpful? A reasonable answer should explain that calendars help people keep track of important events.

**PROJECT 5**

# Apple Math

◎ **Objective** To provide opportunities to classify, count, compare, and measure.

Project 5, along with all other Grade 1 projects, is located at the back of both Volume 1 and Volume 2 of the Grade 1 *Teacher's Lesson Guide*. Use this project during or after Unit 7.

## Adjusting the Activity Ideas

◆ After children make their apple trees, have them write number models for their number stories.

◆ After recording measurements of girth on quarter-sheets of paper, have children arrange the girths of the apples in order from smallest to largest using the recorded measurements.

◆ After children make their apple trees, have children use counters to show how many apples are on their trees. Have partners line up their counters to compare the amounts.

## ELL Support

To provide language support for the Apple Math project, have children compare and contrast the qualities of the apples based on color, shape, and size. Make a list of words that children use to describe the apples on the board for children to refer to as they do the project.

## Writing/Reasoning

Have children draw, write, or verbalize an answer to the following question: How do you use a pan balance to tell which is more? A reasonable answer should suggest that the side with more weight goes down.

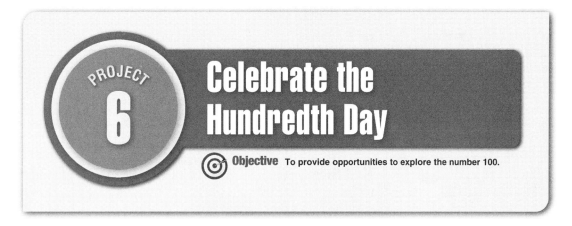

# Celebrate the Hundredth Day

**Objective** To provide opportunities to explore the number 100.

Project 6, along with all other Grade 1 projects, is located at the back of both Volume 1 and Volume 2 of the Grade 1 *Teacher's Lesson Guide*. Use this project on or around the hundredth day of school.

## Adjusting the Activity Ideas

◆ Have children compare the weights of 100 small items from the *Hundreds Museum* using the symbols $<$, $>$, and $=$.

◆ After writing 100 tallies on the board, have children check that they have made 100 tallies using a calculator to count by 5s.

◆ After estimating the number of items in the transparent containers, have children count the items by placing them one by one on the number grid starting at 1. Remind children to put one item in each square.

## ELL Support

To provide language support for the Hundredth Day project, have children discuss the objects they have collected in the *Hundreds Museum*. Have them describe some other items that could be added to the museum and some items that they would not be able to add; for example, they could add 100 jelly beans, but they could not add 100 cars. If several English language learners speak the same language, have them take a minute to discuss the museum in their own language first and then share what they are able to in English.

## Writing/Reasoning

Have children draw, write, or verbalize an answer to the following question: How do you know whether a number is less than 100? A reasonable answer should indicate that the number will have fewer than three digits.

# Weather and Probability

**Objective** To introduce the basic language of probability to describe events.

Project 7, along with all other Grade 1 projects, is located at the back of both Volume 1 and Volume 2 of the Grade 1 *Teacher's Lesson Guide*. Use this project during or after Unit 7.

## Adjusting the Activity Ideas

◆ Ask children to identify words used by weather reporters. List the words on the board. Encourage children to reference the list throughout this project.

◆ After sharing local weather data, have children write and solve number stories about the information.

◆ Make two columns on the board. In one column, list likely events for each season. In the other column, list unlikely events for each season. Allow children to reference this list when they are creating pages for their book.

## ELL Support

To provide language support for the Weather and Probability project, have children use the Math Word Bank template found on page 126 in this handbook. Ask children to write the terms *likely* and *unlikely,* draw a picture representing each term, and write other related words. See page 32 of this handbook for more information.

## Writing/Reasoning

Have children draw, write, or verbalize an answer to the following question: What does unlikely mean? A reasonable answer should explain that if something is unlikely, it probably will not happen.

# A Flea Market

**Objective** To provide opportunities to practice buying-and-selling situations using coins.

Project 8, along with all other Grade 1 projects, is located at the back of both Volume 1 and Volume 2 of the Grade 1 *Teacher's Lesson Guide*. Use this project during or after Unit 8.

## Adjusting the Activity Ideas

◆ Have children use dollar bills to pay for each item they purchase.

◆ Have children make change by counting up from the cost of the item to the amount paid rather than using calculators.

◆ Before the flea market is open, price items with the cost and coin stamps that show the same amount.

## ELL Support

To provide language support for the Flea Market project, make labels with the name for each item along with its price. Keep the labels simple such as *doll, toy car, pencil,* and so on.

## Writing/Reasoning

Have children draw, write, or verbalize an answer to the following question: How do you know whether you have enough money to buy an item? A reasonable answer should include a comparison of the price on the tag and the money available.

# Activities and Ideas for Differentiation

This section highlights Part 1 activities that support differentiation, Part 3 Readiness, Enrichment, Extra Practice, and ELL Support activities built into the lessons of the Grade 1 *Teacher's Lesson Guide,* and specific ideas for vocabulary development and games modifications. Provided in each unit is a chart showing where the Grade-Level Goals emphasized in that unit are addressed throughout the year. Following the chart, there are suggestions for maintaining concepts and skills to ensure that children continue working toward those Grade-Level Goals.

## Contents

Activities and Ideas for Differentiation

# Activities and Ideas for Differentiation

In this unit, children are introduced to a variety of routines that provide them with opportunities to explore, compare, and order numbers. This section summarizes opportunities for supporting multiple learning styles and ability levels. Use these suggestions to develop a differentiation plan for Unit 1.

## Part 1 Activities That Support Differentiation

Below are examples of Unit 1 activities that highlight some of the general instructional strategies that are hallmarks of a differentiated classroom. These strategies will help you support, emphasize, and enhance lesson content to make sure all your children are engaged in the mathematics at the highest possible level. For more information about general differentiation strategies that accommodate the diverse needs of today's classrooms, see the essay on pages 8–16 of this handbook.

| Lesson | Activity | Strategy |
|--------|----------|----------|
| 1•1 | Children use straws to count days. | Modeling concretely |
| 1•2 | Children use the class number line and clues to identify mystery numbers. | Modeling visually |
| 1•5 | Children use a bunny marker to hop on a number line to explore distances. | Modeling physically |
| 1•8 | Children use craft sticks to model making tallies. | Modeling concretely |
| 1•9 | Children use patterns on the calendar to figure out dates one week in the future or past. | Building on prior knowledge |
| 1•10 | Children use counters to compare numbers. | Modeling concretely |

# Vocabulary Development

The list below identifies the Key Vocabulary terms from this unit. The lesson in which each term is defined is indicated next to the term. Some of these terms or their homophones are used outside of mathematics. Consider adding other words as appropriate for developing understanding of the context of the lessons.

Lessons include suggestions for helping English language learners understand and develop vocabulary. For more information, see pages 17–19 of this handbook.

| Key Vocabulary | | |
| --- | --- | --- |
| base-10 blocks (*†base) 1♦11 | geoboard 1♦11 | tally mark 1♦7 |
| †calendar 1♦9 | number line 1♦1 | temperature 1♦12 |
| *date 1♦9 | number story 1♦13 | thermometer 1♦12 |
| *degree 1♦12 | pattern blocks 1♦11 | tool kit (*tool) 1♦3 |
| Exploration 1♦11 | Pattern-Block Template 1♦3 | |
| Fahrenheit 1♦12 | slate 1♦4 | |

\* Discuss the everyday and mathematical meanings of the words that are marked with an asterisk.

† For words marked with a dagger, write the words and their homophones on the board. For example, *base* and *bass* and *calendar* and *calender*. Discuss and clarify the meaning of each.

◆ As each word is introduced in the lesson, write the word on the board and discuss its meaning.

◆ List the words on a Math Word Wall for children to see. As each word is introduced in the lesson, add a picture next to the word on the Word Wall.

◆ Use the vocabulary words regularly when teaching lessons, and encourage children to use the words in their discussions.

 **Games**

Below are suggested Unit 1 game adaptations. For more information about implementing games in a differentiated classroom, see pages 20–25 of this handbook.

**Game: *Monster Squeeze***

**Skill Practiced: Compare whole numbers.** [Number and Numeration Goal 7]

| Modification | Purpose of Modification |
|---|---|
| Players use the range of 0 to 10 on the number line. | Children compare whole numbers less than 10. [Number and Numeration Goal 7] |
| Players provide clues that involve addition or subtraction, for example, "My number is at least 10 more than the monster on the left." | Children use addition and subtraction clues to identify mystery numbers. [Operations and Computation Goal 2] |

**Game: *Penny-Dice Game***

**Skill Practiced: Compare quantities.** [Number and Numeration Goal 7]

| Modification | Purpose of Modification |
|---|---|
| Provide large copies of dice faces so players can match the pennies to the dots. | Children perform rational counts on collections of objects. [Number and Numeration Goal 2] |
| Players use a bank of 50 pennies. When the game ends, they exchange as many pennies for nickels as they can before comparing their totals. | Children make exchanges between pennies and nickels. [Measurement and Reference Frames Goal 2] |

**Game: *Top-It***

**Skill Practiced: Compare whole numbers.** [Number and Numeration Goal 7]

| Modification | Purpose of Modification |
|---|---|
| Each player uses a die instead of number cards. | Children limit the range of numbers and compare whole numbers less than 7. [Number and Numeration Goal 7] |
| For each round, players record their number and their partner's number with tally marks and circle the winning number. | Children write equivalent names for numbers using tallies. [Number and Numeration Goal 6] |

# Math Boxes

Suggestions for using Math Boxes to meet individual needs begin on page 26 of this handbook. There are blank masters for Math Boxes on pages 120–125. Math Boxes are introduced in Unit 2.

# Using Part 3 of the Lessons

Use your professional judgment, along with assessment results, to determine whether the whole class, small groups, or individual children might benefit from these Unit 1 activities. Consider using the Part 3 Planning Master found on page 138 of this handbook to record your plans.

## Readiness Activities

| Lesson | Activity | Purpose of Activity |
|--------|----------|---------------------|
| 1•1 | Make and label number collections. | Gain experience counting objects. [Number and Numeration Goal 1] |
| 1•2 | Sequence sets of numbers. | Gain experience ordering numbers. [Number and Numeration Goal 7] |
| 1•3 | Examine and draw patterns of dots on dice. | Explore number names for dice patterns. [Number and Numeration Goal 6] |
| 1•4 | Count objects and trace the number representing the total number of objects in *Anno's Counting Book*. | Gain experience counting objects and writing numbers. [Number and Numeration Goal 3] |
| 1•5 | Determine 1 more than and 1 less than a set of pennies. | Gain experience counting up and back. [Operations and Computation Goal 1] |
| 1•6 | Match number cards to sets of counters and compare the sets of counters. | Explore comparing numbers. [Number and Numeration Goal 7] |
| 1•7 | Do whisper-and-shout counts by 5s to 40. | Explore skip counting. [Number and Numeration Goal 1] |
| 1•8 | Match number cards and tally cards. | Gain experience with tallying. [Number and Numeration Goal 6] |
| 1•9 | Discuss the words and numbers in birth dates. | Gain experience naming months, days, and years. [Measurement and Reference Frames Goal 4] |
| 1•10 | Compare sets of counters. | Explore comparing quantities. [Number and Numeration Goal 7] |
| 1•11 | Match pattern blocks to color and shape words. | Explore colors and shapes. [Geometry Goal 1] |
| 1•12 | Color temperature zones on the thermometer. | Explore temperature zones. [Measurement and Reference Frames Goal 3] |
| 1•13 | Find number situations represented in picture books. | Gain experience with number recognition. [Operations and Computation Goal 4] |

## Extra Practice Activities

| Lesson | Activity | Purpose of Activity |
|--------|----------|---------------------|
| 1•1 | Skip count and identify shapes in *Minute Math®+* activities. | Practice with counting and shapes. [Geometry Goal 1] |
| 1•2 | Name missing numbers in counts in *Minute Math+* activities. | Practice counting. [Number and Numeration Goal 1] |
| 1•6 | Play *Penny-Dice Game*. | Practice counting and comparing numbers. [Number and Numeration Goal 7] |
| 1•10 | Identify which number is more or less in *Minute Math+* activities. | Practice comparing numbers. [Number and Numeration Goal 7] |

## Enrichment Activities

| Lesson | Activity | Purpose of Activity |
|---|---|---|
| 1◆2 | Create counting books and order the pages. | Explore number relationships. [Number and Numeration Goal 7] |
| 1◆3 | Create patterns using geometric shapes. | Explore geometric patterns. [Geometry Goal 1] |
| 1◆4 | Find the numbers 1–20 hidden in pictures in the book *City By Numbers.* | Explore standard notation for numbers. [Number and Numeration Goal 3] |
| 1◆6 | Use a number line to compare numbers. | Apply understanding of comparing numbers. [Number and Numeration Goal 7] |
| 1◆7 | Make tally marks to record counts. | Apply understanding of making and counting tally marks. [Number and Numeration Goal 6] |
| 1◆8 | Play *Rock, Paper, Scissors.* | Explore tallying as a data-collection strategy. [Data and Chance Goal 1] |
| 1◆9 | Compare two different calendar pages. | Explore features of a calendar. [Measurement and Reference Frames Goal 4] |
| 1◆11 | Make pattern block designs and copy the designs onto a geoboard. | Explore patterns. [Geometry Goal 1] |
| 1◆12 | Make weather booklets illustrating seasonal activities for temperature zones. | Explore temperature and weather. [Measurement and Reference Frames Goal 3] |
| 1◆13 | Write number stories using randomly selected numbers. | Apply understanding of number stories. [Operations and Computation Goal 4] |

## English Language Learners Support Activities

| Lesson | Activity | Purpose of Activity |
|---|---|---|
| 1◆1 | Label the classroom *number line, number grid,* and *calendar.* | Create a language-rich environment. [Number and Numeration Goal 7] |
| 1◆3 | Discuss mathematical *tools.* | Clarify the mathematical and everyday uses of the term. [Measurement and Reference Frames Goal 1] |
| 1◆5 | Add *less* and *more* to the Math Word Bank. | Make connections among and use visuals to represent terms. [Number and Numeration Goal 7] |
| 1◆9 | Discuss the calendar words *day, week, month, year,* and *date* and color code a calendar page. | Use visual models to represent terms. [Measurement and Reference Frames Goal 4] |
| 1◆10 | Compare *larger* and *smaller* numbers and label the ends of a number line. | Use visual models to represent terms. [Number and Numeration Goal 7] |
| 1◆12 | Add *temperature, 80°, 80 degrees,* and *hot* to the Math Word Bank. | Make connections among and use visuals to represent terms. [Measurement and Reference Frames Goal 3] |

# Looking at Grade-Level Goals

*Everyday Mathematics* develops concepts and skills over time. Below is a chart showing where the Grade-Level Goals emphasized in this unit are addressed throughout the year. Use the chart to help you determine which Maintaining Concepts and Skills activities on page 56 to utilize to ensure that children continue working toward these Grade-Level Goals.

● Grade-Level Goal is taught.
◐ Grade-Level Goal is practiced.
○ Grade-Level Goal is not a focus.

| Grade-Level Goals Emphasized in Unit 1 | Unit 1 | 2 | 3 | 4 | 5 | 6 | 7 | 8 | 9 | 10 |
|---|---|---|---|---|---|---|---|---|---|---|
| [Number and Numeration Goal 1] Count on by 1s, 2s, 5s, and 10s past 100 and back by 1s from any number less than 100 with and without number grids, number lines, and calculators. | ● | ● | ● | ● | ● | ● | ◐ | ◐ | ● | ● |
| [Number and Numeration Goal 2] Count collections of objects accurately and reliably; estimate the number of objects in a collection. | ● | ● | ● | ◐ | ● | ● | ● | ◐ | ● | ◐ |
| [Number and Numeration Goal 3] Read, write, and model with manipulatives whole numbers up to 1,000; identify places in such numbers and the values of the digits in those places. | ● | ● | ● | ○ | ● | ◐ | ○ | ● | ● | ◐ |
| [Number and Numeration Goal 6] Use manipulatives, drawings, tally marks, and numerical expressions involving addition and subtraction of 1- or 2-digit numbers to give equivalent names for whole numbers up to 100. | ● | ● | ● | ● | ● | ● | ○ | ◐ | ○ | ○ |
| [Number and Numeration Goal 7] Compare and order whole numbers up to 1,000. | ● | ◐ | ◐ | ● | ● | ● | ● | ● | ◐ | ● |
| [Operations and Computation Goal 1] Demonstrate proficiency with +/− 0, +/− 1, doubles, and sum-equals-ten addition and subtraction facts such as $6 + 4 = 10$ and $10 − 7 = 3$. | ● | ● | ● | ● | ● | ● | ● | ◐ | ● | ● |
| [Operations and Computation Goal 2] Use manipulatives, number grids, tally marks, mental arithmetic, and calculators to solve problems involving the addition and subtraction of 1-digit whole numbers with 1- or 2-digit whole numbers; calculate and compare the values of combinations of coins. | ● | ● | ● | ● | ● | ● | ○ | ◐ | ○ | ◐ |
| [Data and Chance Goal 1] Collect and organize data to create tally charts, tables, bar graphs, and line plots. | ● | ○ | ○ | ○ | ○ | ● | ○ | ◐ | ○ | ◐ |
| [Data and Chance Goal 2] Use graphs to answer simple questions and draw conclusions; find the maximum and minimum of a data set. | ● | ◐ | ◐ | ◐ | ○ | ◐ | ◐ | ◐ | ◐ | ◐ |
| [Geometry Goal 1] Identify and describe plane and solid figures including circles, triangles, squares, rectangles, spheres, cylinders, rectangular prisms, pyramids, cones, and cubes. | ● | ◐ | ◐ | ○ | ○ | ● | ◐ | ◐ | ◐ | ◐ |
| [Patterns, Functions, and Algebra Goal 1] Extend, describe, and create numeric, visual, and concrete patterns; solve problems involving function machines, "What's My Rule?" tables, and Frames-and-Arrows diagrams. | ● | ● | ● | ◐ | ◐ | ◐ | ● | ◐ | ● | ◐ |

# Maintaining Concepts and Skills

All of the goals addressed in this unit will be addressed again in later units. Here are several suggestions for maintaining concepts and skills until they are formally revisited.

### Number and Numeration Goal 1

◆ Have children count forward and backward on the number grid by 2s, 5s, and 10s. If you have not already done so, consider indicating these counts on the number line; for example, draw circles around counts by 2, squares around counts by 5, and triangles around counts by 10.

◆ Have children, on the number grid, lightly shade counts by 2 in one color, counts by 5 in a second color, and counts by 10 in both colors.

### Number and Numeration Goal 3

◆ Have children trace numbers in *Anno's Counting Book*. See the Readiness activity in Lesson 1-4 for more information.

### Number and Numeration Goal 6

◆ Have children match number cards and tally cards. See the Readiness activity in Lesson 1-8 for more information.

◆ Make a tally of the number of children whenever you do a class count, such as a lunch count.

### Number and Numeration Goal 7

◆ Have children play *Top-It* varying the range of numbers and difficulty as appropriate.

◆ Have children play *Monster Squeeze* varying the range of numbers as appropriate.

◆ Have children compare sets of counters. See the Readiness activity in Lesson 1-10 for more information.

# Assessment

See page 54 in the *Assessment Handbook* for modifications to the written portion of the Unit 1 Progress Check.

Additionally, see pages 55–59 for modifications to the open-response task and selected child work samples.

# Unit 2 — Activities and Ideas for Differentiation

In this unit, children work with time and money concepts. Children are also introduced to number stories and number models. This section summarizes opportunities for supporting multiple learning styles and ability levels. Use these suggestions to develop a differentiation plan for Unit 2.

## Part 1 Activities That Support Differentiation

Below are examples of Unit 2 activities that highlight some of the general instructional strategies that are hallmarks of a differentiated classroom. These strategies will help you support, emphasize, and enhance lesson content to make sure all your children are engaged in the mathematics at the highest possible level. For more information about general differentiation strategies that accommodate the diverse needs of today's classrooms, see the essay on pages 8–16 of this handbook.

| Lesson | Activity | Strategy |
|--------|----------|----------|
| 2•1 | Use the number grid to provide a visual reference for skip counting. | Modeling visually |
| 2•3 | Children predict how many pennies out of 10 are hidden based on the number of pennies showing. | Modeling concretely |
| 2•5 | Use the demonstration clock to show hour and minute hands. | Modeling visually |
| 2•6 | Children make personal clocks to explore the characteristics of the hour and minute hands. | Modeling physically |
| 2•7 | Children sort dominoes according to the number of dots. | Modeling visually |
| 2•12 | Model a change-to-less diagram by taking a collection of standing paper cups and tipping some over to decrease the number of standing cups. | Modeling physically |

# Vocabulary Development

The list below identifies the Key Vocabulary terms from this unit. The lesson in which each term is defined is indicated next to the term. Some of these terms or their homophones are used outside of mathematics. Consider adding other words as appropriate for developing understanding of the context of the lessons.

Lessons include suggestions for helping English language learners understand and develop vocabulary. For more information, see pages 17–19 of this handbook.

---

## Key Vocabulary

| | | |
|---|---|---|
| †add **2♦11** | Math Boxes **2♦3** | penny **2♦8** |
| A.M. **2♦6** | midnight **2♦6** | plus **2♦11** |
| analog clock **2♦5** | minus **2♦12** | P.M. **2♦6** |
| †cent **2♦8** | minute hand (*hand) **2♦5** | *ruler **2♦7** |
| clockwise **2♦6** | nickel **2♦9** | subtract **2♦12** |
| estimate **2♦5** | noon **2♦6** | *unit **2♦4** |
| hour hand (†hour) **2♦5** | number grid **2♦1** | unit box (*box) **2♦4** |
| is equal to **2♦11** | number model (*model) **2♦11** | |

---

* Discuss the everyday and mathematical meanings of the words that are marked with an asterisk.

† For words marked with a dagger, write the words and their homophones on the board. For example, *add* and *ad; cent, sent,* and *scent;* and *hour* and *our.* Discuss and clarify the meaning of each.

◆ As each word is introduced in the lesson, write the word on the board and discuss its meaning.

◆ List the words on a Math Word Wall for children to see. As each word is introduced in the lesson, add a picture next to the word on the Word Wall.

◆ Use the vocabulary words regularly when teaching lessons, and encourage children to use the words in their discussions.

 **Games**

Below are suggested Unit 2 game adaptations. For more information about implementing games in a differentiated classroom, see pages 20–25 of this handbook.

**Game: *Penny-Nickel Exchange***

**Skill Practiced: Exchange pennies for nickels.** [Measurement and Reference Frames Goal 2]

| Modification | Purpose of Modification |
|---|---|
| Players use a bank of 50 pennies. Instead of making exchanges during the game, children play until all pennies are gone. At the end of the game, players count their pennies and then exchange the pennies for nickels. Players recalculate their total after the exchanges. | Children calculate the value of collections of pennies. [Operations and Computation Goal 2] |
| If a player rolls a 1, he or she collects a nickel instead of a penny and records the total at the end of each round. | Children calculate the value of penny and nickel combinations. [Operations and Computation Goal 2] |

**Game: *High Roller***

**Skill Practiced: Find sums.** [Operations and Computation Goal 2]

| Modification | Purpose of Modification |
|---|---|
| For each round, players record the larger of the two numbers shown on the dice. This is the total for the round. | Children limit the range of numbers they are comparing to whole numbers less than 7. [Number and Numeration Goal 7] |
| Players keep the die with the larger number, double that number, roll the other die again, and add that number to the double to score each round. | Children practice doubles facts. [Operations and Computation Goal 1] |

**Game: *Coin Top-It***

**Skill Practiced: Calculate and compare the value of coin combinations.** [Measurement and Reference Frames Goal 2]

| Modification | Purpose of Modification |
|---|---|
| Players make a set of cards that has only pennies or a set that has only nickels. They count by 1s or by 5s to find the total value of the card. | Children calculate and compare the value of coin combinations involving only one kind of coin. [Measurement and Reference Frames Goal 2] |
| Players draw two coin cards on every turn. They calculate the total for all of the coins pictured on both cards. They add a bonus point if the total can be represented with only nickels (a multiple of 5). | Children calculate and compare the value of coin combinations and identify multiples of 5. [Measurement and Reference Frames Goal 2] |

 **Math Boxes**

Suggestions for using Math Boxes to meet individual needs begin on page 26 of this handbook. There are blank masters for Math Boxes on pages 120–125. Math Boxes are introduced in this unit.

# Using Part 3 of the Lessons

Use your professional judgment, along with assessment results, to determine whether the whole class, small groups, or individual children might benefit from these Unit 2 activities. Consider using the Part 3 Planning Master found on page 138 of this handbook to record your plans.

## Readiness Activities

| Lesson | Activity | Purpose of Activity |
|--------|----------|---------------------|
| 2◆1 | Color return sweeps on the number grid. | Provide visual clues for navigating the number grid. [Number and Numeration Goal 7] |
| 2◆2 | Sort numbers into two categories. | Explore numbers. [Number and Numeration Goal 6] |
| 2◆3 | Line up pennies on the number line to count them. | Gain experience with counting. [Number and Numeration Goal 6] |
| 2◆4 | Match number labels to collections of items. | Gain experience counting objects. [Number and Numeration Goal 2] |
| 2◆6 | Predict things that can be done in a second and a minute; then test the predictions. | Explore the duration of seconds and minutes. [Measurement and Reference Frames Goal 4] |
| 2◆7 | Compare lengths of string. | Explore linear measure. [Measurement and Reference Frames Goal 1] |
| 2◆8 | Count pennies by placing them on the number grid. | Gain experience with counting. [Number and Numeration Goal 2] |
| 2◆9 | Count pennies using tally marks. | Explore skip counting by 5s. [Number and Numeration Goal 1] |
| 2◆10 | Identify pennies and nickels by touch. | Explore differences between pennies and nickels. [Measurement and Reference Frames Goal 2] |
| 2◆11 | Model and solve addition number stories using craft sticks. | Gain experience with addition number stories. [Operations and Computation Goal 2] |
| 2◆12 | Count backward from 20 using pennies. | Explore counting. [Number and Numeration Goal 1] |
| 2◆13 | Solve number stories by acting them out with number and operation cards. | Gain experience with addition and subtraction. [Operations and Computation Goal 2; Patterns, Functions, and Algebra Goal 2] |

## English Language Learners Support Activities

| Lesson | Activity | Purpose of Activity |
|--------|----------|---------------------|
| 2◆2 | Describe the kinds of numbers in the Numbers All Around Museum. | Make connections between mathematics and everyday life; discuss new mathematical ideas. [Number and Numeration Goal 3] |
| 2◆5 | Add *minute hand* and *hour hand* to the Math Word Bank. | Make connections among and use visuals to represent terms. [Measurement and Reference Frames Goal 4] |
| 2◆6 | Add *noon* and *midnight* to the Math Word Bank. | Make connections among and use visuals to represent terms. [Measurement and Reference Frames Goal 4] |
| 2◆8 | Add *cent* to the Math Word Bank. | Make connections among and use visuals to represent terms. [Measurement and Reference Frames Goal 2] |
| 2◆11 | Add *add* to the Math Word Bank. | Make connections among and use visuals to represent terms. [Operations and Computation Goal 2] |
| 2◆12 | Add *subtract* to the Math Word Bank. | Make connections among and use visuals to represent terms. [Operations and Computation Goal 2] |

# Enrichment Activities

| Lesson | Activity | Purpose of Activity |
|--------|----------|---------------------|
| 2◆1 | Count up and back by 10s on the number grid. | Explore navigating the number grid. [Number and Numeration Goal 7] |
| 2◆2 | Write combinations for the last four digits of a mystery phone number. | Explore number combinations. [Number and Numeration Goal 3] |
| 2◆3 | Do *Two-Fisted Penny Addition* with 10 pennies. | Explore complements of 10. [Number and Numeration Goal 6] |
| 2◆5 | Illustrate daily activities according to the time of day. | Apply understanding of time. [Measurement and Reference Frames Goal 4] |
| 2◆6 | Calculate elapsed time in hours. | Apply understanding of time. [Measurement and Reference Frames Goal 4] |
| 2◆7 | Draw pattern-block shapes and compare the lengths of the sides of the shapes. | Explore length. [Measurement and Reference Frames Goal 1] |
| 2◆8 | Order pennies by mint date. | Explore pennies. [Measurement and Reference Frames Goal 2] |
| 2◆9 | Predict how many nickels can be exchanged for a pile of pennies, then check predictions. | Explore penny-nickel exchanges. [Measurement and Reference Frames Goal 2] |
| 2◆10 | Make coin combinations for given amounts using pennies and nickels. | Apply understanding of the value of pennies and nickels. [Operations and Computation Goal 2] |
| 2◆11 | Grab and count handfuls of pennies and nickels. | Explore estimating totals. [Operations and Computation Goal 3] |
| 2◆12 | Play *Who Am I Thinking Of?* | Gain experience with number models. [Patterns, Functions, and Algebra Goal 2] |
| 2◆13 | Run and shop at a classroom store. | Explore money exchanges. [Measurement and Reference Frames Goal 2] |

# Extra Practice Activities

| Lesson | Activity | Purpose of Activity |
|--------|----------|---------------------|
| 2◆4 | Draw a number of items and label with appropriate units. | Practice counting objects. [Number and Numeration Goal 2] |
| 2◆6 | Tell time on an analog clock. | Practice telling time. [Measurement and Reference Frames Goal 4] |
| 2◆8 | Play *Penny-Dice Game.* | Compare numbers. [Number and Numeration Goal 7] |
| 2◆13 | Read *Twenty Is Too Many* and write a number model for the story. | Practice writing number stories. [Operations and Computation Goal 2] |

# Looking at Grade-Level Goals

*Everyday Mathematics* develops concepts and skills over time. Below is a chart showing where the Grade-Level Goals emphasized in this unit are addressed throughout the year. Use the chart to help you determine which Maintaining Concepts and Skills activities on page 63 to utilize to ensure that children continue working toward these Grade-Level Goals.

Legend:
- ● Grade-Level Goal is taught.
- ◐ Grade-Level Goal is practiced.
- ○ Grade-Level Goal is not a focus.

## Grade-Level Goals Emphasized in Unit 2

| Goal | 1 | 2 | 3 | 4 | 5 | 6 | 7 | 8 | 9 | 10 |
|---|---|---|---|---|---|---|---|---|---|---|
| [Number and Numeration Goal 1] Count on by 1s, 2s, 5s, and 10s past 100 and back by 1s from any number less than 100 with and without number grids, number lines, and calculators. | ● | ● | ● | ● | ◐ | ● | ◐ | ◐ | ● | ◐ |
| [Number and Numeration Goal 2] Count collections of objects accurately and reliably; estimate the number of objects in a collection. | ● | ● | ● | ◐ | ● | ● | ◐ | ◐ | ● | ◐ |
| [Number and Numeration Goal 3] Read, write, and model with manipulatives whole numbers up to 1,000; identify places in such numbers and the values of the digits in those places. | ● | ● | ● | ○ | ● | ◐ | ● | ◐ | ● | ◐ |
| [Number and Numeration Goal 6] Use manipulatives, drawings, tally marks, and numerical expressions involving addition and subtraction of 1- or 2-digit numbers to give equivalent names for whole numbers up to 100. | ● | ● | ◐ | ● | ● | ◐ | ○ | ◐ | ○ | ◐ |
| [Number and Numeration Goal 7] Compare and order whole numbers up to 1,000. | ● | ● | ● | ● | ● | ● | ○ | ● | ● | ◐ |
| [Operations and Computation Goal 2] Use manipulatives, number grids, tally marks, mental arithmetic, and calculators to solve problems involving the addition and subtraction of 1-digit whole numbers with 1- or 2-digit whole numbers; calculate and compare the values of combinations of coins. | ● | ● | ● | ● | ● | ● | ● | ● | ● | ● |
| [Measurement and Reference Frames Goal 2] Know and compare the value of pennies, nickels, dimes, quarters, and dollar bills; make exchanges between coins. | ○ | ● | ● | ◐ | ○ | ○ | ● | ◐ | ● | ◐ |
| [Measurement and Reference Frames Goal 4] Use a calendar to identify days, weeks, months, and dates; tell and show time to the nearest half and quarter hour on an analog clock. | ○ | ● | ● | ● | ○ | ○ | ○ | ○ | ● | ● |
| [Patterns, Functions, and Algebra Goal 2] Read, write, and explain expressions and number sentences using the symbols +, −, and = and the symbols > and < with cues; solve equations involving addition and subtraction. | ○ | ● | ● | ○ | ● | ● | ● | ● | ● | ◐ |

Unit

# Maintaining Concepts and Skills

All of the goals addressed in this unit will be addressed again in later units. Here are several suggestions for maintaining concepts and skills until they are formally revisited.

### Number and Numeration Goal 1

◆ Have children count pennies to practice counting by 1s and count nickels to practice counting by 5s.

◆ Have children place nickels on the number grid at intervals of 5; for example, the first nickel goes on 5, the second nickel goes on 10, the third nickel goes on 15, and so on. Children move along the number grid and point to the nickels as they count.

### Number and Numeration Goal 6

◆ Have children play *Top-It* and record the number on their card in tallies for each round.

### Operations and Computation Goal 2

◆ Have children play *High Roller* for addition and *Coin Top-It* for finding the value of combinations of pennies and nickels.

◆ Have children act out number stories. See the Readiness activity in Lesson 2-11 for more information.

### Measurement and Reference Frames Goal 4

◆ Have children predict things that can be done in a second or a minute. See the Readiness activity in Lesson 2-6 for more information.

# Assessment

See page 62 in the *Assessment Handbook* for modifications to the written portion of the Unit 2 Progress Check.

Additionally, see pages 63–67 for modifications to the open-response task and selected child work samples.

# Activities and Ideas for Differentiation

In this unit, children work with patterns in a variety of contexts, further explore telling time, and continue to calculate totals for coin combinations. This section summarizes opportunities for supporting multiple learning styles and ability levels. Use these suggestions to develop a differentiation plan for Unit 3.

## Part 1 Activities That Support Differentiation

Below are examples of Unit 3 activities that highlight some of the general instructional strategies that are hallmarks of a differentiated classroom. These strategies will help you support, emphasize, and enhance lesson content to make sure all your children are engaged in the mathematics at the highest possible level. For more information about general differentiation strategies that accommodate the diverse needs of today's classrooms, see the essay on pages 8–16 of this handbook.

| Lesson | Activity | Strategy |
|--------|----------|----------|
| 3•1 | Children make craft-stick patterns. | Modeling concretely |
| 3•3 | Mark skip counts on the number grid with color dots. | Modeling visually |
| 3•4 | Children sort dominoes according to whether they have an odd or even number of dots. | Modeling visually |
| 3•6 | Children use the number line to model subtraction. | Modeling visually |
| 3•10 | Children skip count on a calculator. | Modeling physically |
| 3•13 | Children make a line plot using stick-on notes and discuss features of the resulting line plot. | Modeling concretely |

# Vocabulary Development

The list below identifies the Key Vocabulary terms from this unit. The lesson in which each term is defined is indicated next to the term. Some of these terms or their homophones are used outside of mathematics. Consider adding other words as appropriate for developing understanding of the context of the lessons.

Lessons include suggestions for helping English language learners understand and develop vocabulary. For more information, see pages 17–19 of this handbook.

| Key Vocabulary | | |
|---|---|---|
| arrow **3♦8** | even number **3♦2** | number line **3♦5** |
| arrow rule (*rule) **3♦8** | *frame **3♦8** | odd number (*odd) **3♦2** |
| column **3♦3** | Frames-and-Arrows diagram **3♦8** | pattern **3♦1** |
| decimal point (*point) **3♦11** | half-past (the hour) (†past) **3♦7** | *program **3♦10** |
| dime **3♦11** | line plot (*plot) **3♦13** | *†row **3♦3** |
| dollars-and-cents notation **3♦11** | negative number **3♦5** | |

\* Discuss the everyday and mathematical meanings of the words that are marked with an asterisk.

† For the words marked with a dagger, write the words and their homophones on the board. For example, *past* and *passed* and *row* and *roe*. Discuss and clarify the meaning of each.

◆ As each word is introduced in the lesson, write the word on the board and discuss its meaning.

◆ List the words on a Math Word Wall for children to see. As each word is introduced in the lesson, add a picture next to the word on the Word Wall.

◆ Use the vocabulary words regularly when teaching lessons, and encourage children to use the words in their discussions.

 **Games**

Below are suggested Unit 3 game adaptations. For more information about implementing games in a differentiated classroom, see pages 20–25 of this handbook.

**Game: *Before and After***

**Skill Practiced: Counting forward and backward by 1s.** [Number and Numeration Goal 1]

| Modification | Purpose of Modification |
|---|---|
| Players choose to always play 1 more or 1 less during a game. To start, both "number-side up" cards on the table should be 1s if playing 1 more or 10s if playing 1 less. | Children count forward or backward by 1s. [Number and Numeration Goal 1] |
| Players count by 2s, playing the card that is 2 more or 2 less than the number showing. Begin with one even and one odd number-side up card. After playing a few rounds, have players discuss the role of even and odd numbers in the game. | Children skip count forward and backward by 2s. [Number and Numeration Goal 1] |

**Game: *Coin-Dice***

**Skill Practiced: Make coin exchanges.** [Measurement and Reference Frames Goal 2]

| Modification | Purpose of Modification |
|---|---|
| At the end of the game, players make exchanges. They count their pennies, record their totals, and then exchange for nickels. They calculate and record their totals again and exchange for dimes. They calculate and then record their final totals. | Children make simple coin exchanges. [Measurement and Reference Frames Goal 2] |
| Players roll two dice. On each turn, they pick up the number of pennies indicated by the smaller number and the number of nickels indicated by the larger number. They exchange for dimes if possible. | Children calculate the value of coin combinations. [Operations and Computation Goal 2] |

**Game: *Domino Top-It***

**Skill Practiced: Find sums and compare numbers.** [Number and Numeration Goal 7; Operations and Computation Goal 2]

| Modification | Purpose of Modification |
|---|---|
| Players take the number of counters indicated on each half of the domino and then find the total. | Children find sums for domino halves using counters. [Operations and Computation Goal 2] |
| Players draw two dominoes on each turn. They record an addition number sentence and find the sum for the two dominoes. The addends in their number sentence may represent domino halves (4 addends) or domino sums (2 addends). | Children find sums for numbers represented on dominoes. [Operations and Computation Goal 2] |

 **Math Boxes**

Suggestions for using Math Boxes to meet individual needs begin on page 26 of this handbook. There are blank masters for Math Boxes on pages 120–125.

# Using Part 3 of the Lessons

Use your professional judgment, along with assessment results, to determine whether the whole class, small groups, or individual children might benefit from these Unit 3 activities. Consider using the Part 3 Planning Master found on page 138 of this handbook to record your plans.

## Readiness Activities

| Lesson | Activity | Purpose of Activity |
|---|---|---|
| 3♦1 | Shade shapes for patterns. | Explore patterns. [Patterns, Functions, and Algebra Goal 1] |
| 3♦2 | Act out even and odd numbers with groups of children. | Explore even and odd numbers. [Number and Numeration Goal 5] |
| 3♦3 | Do interrupted skip counting. | Explore skip counting. [Number and Numeration Goal 1] |
| 3♦4 | Identify and discuss patterns in dice dots. | Explore even and odd numbers. [Number and Numeration Goal 5] |
| 3♦5 | Count hops on a number line. | Explore navigating along a number line. [Number and Numeration Goal 1] |
| 3♦6 | Write dictated number models. | Gain experience using +, −, and = to write number models. [Patterns, Functions, and Algebra Goal 2] |
| 3♦7 | Show times on an analog clock for *Hickory Dickory Dock.* | Gain experience telling time to the hour. [Measurement and Reference Frames Goal 4] |
| 3♦8 | Show counting patterns on a number line. | Explore how the Frames-and-Arrows sequence is related to counting on a number line. [Patterns, Functions, and Algebra Goal 1] |
| 3♦9 | Identify patterns on a number line. | Explore how to find the rule in Frames-and-Arrows sequences. [Patterns, Functions, and Algebra Goal 1] |
| 3♦11 | Do stop-and-start counting by 10s, 5s, and 1s. | Explore counting. [Number and Numeration Goal 1] |
| 3♦12 | Count collections of the same kind of coins. | Gain experience counting coins. [Measurement and Reference Frames Goal 2] |
| 3♦13 | Show tallies with craft sticks. | Gain experience with making tally marks. [Data and Chance Goal 1] |
| 3♦14 | Match domino dots with number cards. | Explore solving parts-and-total problems. [Operations and Computation Goal 4] |

## English Language Learners Support Activities

| Lesson | Activity | Purpose of Activity |
|---|---|---|
| 3♦2 | Add *even* and *odd* to the Math Word Bank. | Make connections among and use visuals to represent terms. [Number and Numeration Goal 5] |
| 3♦3 | Add *row, column,* and *diagonal* to the Math Word Bank. | Make connections among and use visuals to represent terms. [Patterns, Functions, and Algebra Goal 1] |
| 3♦7 | Label and color clocks at *half-past.* | Create a language-rich environment. [Measurement and Reference Frames Goal 4] |
| 3♦11 | Add *dime,* ⑩, *10¢,* and *$0.10* to the Math Word Bank. | Make connections among and use visuals to represent terms. [Measurement and Reference Frames Goal 2] |
| 3♦13 | Add *line plot* to the Math Word Bank. | Make connections among and use visuals to represent terms. [Data and Chance Goal 1] |

## Enrichment Activities

| Lesson | Activity | Purpose of Activity |
|---|---|---|
| 3•1 | Translate shape patterns into letter patterns. | Explore naming patterns. [Patterns, Functions, and Algebra Goal 1] |
| 3•2 | Identify even and odd numbers in skip counts. | Explore even and odd numbers. [Number and Numeration Goal 5] |
| 3•3 | Count by 3s on a number grid and discuss the pattern. | Explore number-grid patterns. [Patterns, Functions, and Algebra Goal 1] |
| 3•5 | Fill in missing numbers on a negative number line. | Explore number sequences. [Number and Numeration Goal 1] |
| 3•6 | Tell number stories and model solutions with pennies. | Explore solving number stories. [Operations and Computation Goal 2] |
| 3•7 | Order clocks by the displayed times. | Explore telling time. [Measurement and Reference Frames Goal 4] |
| 3•8 | Write Frames-and-Arrows problems. | Apply understanding of rules and patterns. [Patterns, Functions, and Algebra Goal 1] |
| 3•9 | Complete Frames-and-Arrows diagrams for number-grid patterns. | Explore rules and patterns. [Patterns, Functions, and Algebra Goal 1] |
| 3•10 | Skip count on a calculator to check Frames-and-Arrows problems. | Explore counting on calculators. [Number and Numeration Goal 1] |
| 3•12 | Make exchanges for collections of coins. | Explore counting coins. [Measurement and Reference Frames Goal 2] |
| 3•13 | Create a line plot with previously collected data. | Explore line plots. [Data and Chance Goal 1] |
| 3•14 | Find the sums for domino parts and tell whether the sums are odd or even. | Explore even and odd numbers. [Number and Numeration Goal 5] |

## Extra Practice Activities

| Lesson | Activity | Purpose of Activity |
|---|---|---|
| 3•1 | Read *Pattern Bugs* and write a word pattern. | Practice making patterns. [Patterns, Functions, and Algebra Goal 1] |
| 3•2 | Read *Missing Mittens* and record a number that is even or odd. | Practice with even and odd numbers. [Number and Numeration Goal 5] |
| 3•4 | Identify and form shapes in *Minute Math+* activities. | Practice with shapes. [Geometry Goal 1] |
| 3•5 | Read *Two Ways to Count to Ten* and record three ways to count to 10. | Practice skip counting. [Number and Numeration Goal 1] |
| 3•6 | Play *Bunny Hop*. | Practice counting on the number line. [Number and Numeration Goal 1] |
| 3•10 | Skip count up and back on a number line. | Practice counting on the number line. [Number and Numeration Goal 1] |
| 3•11 | Make coin exchanges and find coin equivalences in *Minute Math+* activities. | Practice with coin values. [Measurement and Reference Frames Goal 2] |

# Looking at Grade-Level Goals

*Everyday Mathematics* develops concepts and skills over time. Below is a chart showing where the Grade-Level Goals emphasized in this unit are addressed throughout the year. Use the chart to help you determine which Maintaining Concepts and Skills activities on page 70 to utilize to ensure that children continue working toward these Grade-Level Goals.

- ● Grade-Level Goal is taught.
- ◑ Grade-Level Goal is practiced.
- ○ Grade-Level Goal is not a focus.

| Grade-Level Goals Emphasized in Unit 3 | 1 | 2 | 3 | 4 | 5 | 6 | 7 | 8 | 9 | 10 |
|---|---|---|---|---|---|---|---|---|---|---|
| [Number and Numeration Goal 1] Count on by 1s, 2s, 5s, and 10s past 100 and back by 1s from any number less than 100 with and without number grids, number lines, and calculators. | ● | ● | ● | ● | ● | ● | ◑ | ● | ● | ● |
| [Number and Numeration Goal 2] Count collections of objects accurately and reliably; estimate the number of objects in a collection. | ● | ● | ● | ◑ | ● | ● | ◑ | ● | ● | ○ |
| [Number and Numeration Goal 3] Read, write, and model with manipulatives whole numbers up to 1,000; identify places in such numbers and the values of the digits in those places. | ● | ● | ● | ◑ | ● | ● | ● | ● | ● | ◑ |
| [Number and Numeration Goal 5] Use manipulatives to identify and model odd and even numbers. | ○ | ○ | ● | ○ | ● | ● | ○ | ○ | ○ | ○ |
| [Number and Numeration Goal 7] Compare and order whole numbers up to 1,000. | ● | ● | ● | ◑ | ● | ● | ● | ● | ● | ◑ |
| [Operations and Computation Goal 2] Use manipulatives, number grids, tally marks, mental arithmetic, and calculators to solve problems involving the addition and subtraction of 1-digit whole numbers with 1- or 2-digit whole numbers; calculate and compare the values of combinations of coins. | ● | ● | ● | ● | ● | ● | ● | ● | ● | ● |
| [Operations and Computation Goal 3] Estimate reasonableness of answers to basic fact problems (e.g., Will 7 + 8 be more or less than 10?). | ○ | ○ | ● | ○ | ◑ | ◑ | ○ | ◑ | ● | ◑ |
| [Measurement and Reference Frames Goal 2] Know and compare the value of pennies, nickels, dimes, quarters, and dollar bills; make exchanges between coins. | ○ | ● | ● | ● | ○ | ○ | ● | ● | ● | ● |
| [Patterns, Functions, and Algebra Goal 1] Extend, describe, and create numeric, visual, and concrete patterns; solve problems involving function machines, "What's My Rule?" tables, and Frames-and-Arrows diagrams. | ● | ◑ | ● | ● | ● | ● | ● | ● | ● | ● |
| [Patterns, Functions, and Algebra Goal 2] Read, write, and explain expressions and number sentences using the symbols +, −, and = and the symbols > and < with cues; solve equations involving addition and subtraction. | ○ | ● | ● | ◑ | ● | ● | ● | ● | ● | ◑ |

# Maintaining Concepts and Skills

All of the goals addressed in this unit will be addressed again in later units. Here are several suggestions for maintaining concepts and skills until they are formally revisited.

### Number and Numeration Goal 1

◆ Have children play *Before-and-After*.

◆ Have children do interrupted skip counts. See the Readiness activity in Lesson 3-3 for more information.

◆ Continue to practice counts by 1s, 2s, and 5s on the number grid.

### Number and Numeration Goal 7

◆ Have children play *Top-It* and *Domino Top-It*.

### Operations and Computation Goal 2

◆ Have children play *Domino Top-It* and *Penny Grab* to practice finding sums.

◆ Have children do stop-and-start counting by 10s, 5s, and 1s to help with counting coin combinations.

### Patterns, Functions, and Algebra Goal 1

◆ Have children shade shapes to complete and continue patterns. See the Readiness activity in Lesson 3-1 for more information.

◆ Use Frames-and-Arrows masters A and B on pages 128 and 129 of this handbook to create practice problems.

## Assessment

See page 70 in the *Assessment Handbook* for modifications to the written portion of the Unit 3 Progress Check.

Additionally, see pages 71–75 for modifications to the open-response task and selected child work samples.

# Unit 4
# Activities and Ideas for Differentiation

In this unit, children explore linear measure with standard and nonstandard units, fact power, and patterns in number grids. This section summarizes opportunities for supporting multiple learning styles and ability levels. Use these suggestions to develop a differentiation plan for Unit 4.

## Part 1 Activities That Support Differentiation

Below are examples of Unit 4 activities that highlight some of the general instructional strategies that are hallmarks of a differentiated classroom. These strategies will help you support, emphasize, and enhance lesson content to make sure all your children are engaged in the mathematics at the highest possible level. For more information about general differentiation strategies that accommodate the diverse needs of today's classrooms, see the essay on pages 8–16 of this handbook.

| Lesson | Activity | Strategy |
|--------|----------|----------|
| 4◆2 | Children find objects in the room that are taller than, shorter than, or about the same height as they are. | Connecting to everyday life |
| 4◆3 | Children measure the length of objects in the room using tracings of their feet. | Modeling concretely |
| 4◆4 | Children measure the length of objects using 1-inch squares. | Modeling concretely |
| 4◆7 | Children build shapes on the geoboard to informally explore the attributes of the shapes. | Modeling concretely |
| 4◆9 | Children draw pictures on a timeline to represent events. | Modeling visually |
| 4◆12 | Children record addition facts where the addends are domino halves and the sum is the total of the dots on the domino. | Modeling visually |

# Vocabulary Development

The list below identifies the Key Vocabulary terms from this unit. The lesson in which each term is defined is indicated next to the term. Some of these terms or their homophones are used outside of mathematics. Consider adding other words as appropriate for developing understanding of the context of the lessons.

Lessons include suggestions for helping English language learners understand and develop vocabulary. For more information, see pages 17–19 of this handbook.

---

### Key Vocabulary

| | | |
|---|---|---|
| addition facts **4◆11** | *hand **4◆2** | standard foot **4◆3** |
| arm span **4◆2** | half-past (the hour) (†past) **4◆8** | †sum **4◆11** |
| bar graph (*bar) **4◆7** | hand span **4◆2** | tape measure **4◆6** |
| cubit **4◆2** | in. **4◆4** | temperature **4◆1** |
| *degree **4◆1** | inch **4◆4** | thermometer **4◆1** |
| *digit **4◆2** | length **4◆2** | timeline **4◆9** |
| estimate **4◆5** | Math Message **4◆1** | typical **4◆7** |
| fact power (*power) **4◆11** | measure **4◆2** | *unit **4◆2** |
| Fahrenheit **4◆1** | quarter-after, quarter-past (the hour) (*quarter) **4◆8** | *yard **4◆2** |
| *†feet **4◆3** | | |
| *foot **4◆3** | quarter-before, quarter-to (the hour) **4◆8** | |

---

★ Discuss the everyday and mathematical meanings of the words that are marked with an asterisk.

† For words marked with a dagger, write the words and their homophones on the board. For example, *feet* and *feat; past* and *passed;* and *sum* and *some.* Discuss and clarify the meaning of each.

◆ As each word is introduced in the lesson, write the word on the board and discuss its meaning.

◆ List the words on a Math Word Wall for children to see. As each word is introduced in the lesson, add a picture next to the word on the Word Wall.

◆ Use the vocabulary words regularly when teaching lessons, and encourage children to use the words in their discussions.

 **Games**

Below are suggested Unit 4 game adaptations. For more information about implementing games in a differentiated classroom, see pages 20–25 of this handbook.

### Game: *Dime - Nickel - Penny Grab*

**Skill Practiced: Calculate the values of coin combinations.** [Operations and Computation Goal 2]

| Modification | Purpose of Modification |
|---|---|
| Players grab one handful of pennies and one handful of dimes. They count the dimes first and then count on by 1s for the pennies to find the totals. | Children calculate the values of coin combinations involving pennies and dimes. [Operations and Computation Goal 2] |
| Players begin with a bank that has 20 dimes, 16 nickels, and 20 pennies. Players calculate and record the total value of the coins they grab. If the value is greater than $1, they get a bonus of 10 points. | Children calculate the values of coin combinations greater than one dollar. [Operations and Computation Goal 2] |

### Game: *Time Match*

**Skill Practiced: Tell time.** [Measurement and Reference Frames Goal 4]

| Modification | Purpose of Modification |
|---|---|
| Players use only the cards showing or telling time to the hour. Label your classroom clock with "o'clock" and "half-past" to serve as a reference. | Children tell time to the hour. [Measurement and Reference Frames Goal 4] |
| Players receive a bonus point if they can tell what time it would be one-half hour later than the time shown on 1 of the cards they win. | Children tell time and find elapsed time for a half-hour later. [Measurement and Reference Frames Goal 4] |

### Game: *Penny Plate*

**Skill Practiced: Find sums of 10.** [Operations and Computation Goal 1]

| Modification | Purpose of Modification |
|---|---|
| The player guessing how many pennies are under the plate uses 10 counters to model the problem. | Children find sums of 10 using a concrete model. [Operations and Computation Goal 1] |
| The player hiding the pennies can choose between 10 and 20 pennies and report the total number of pennies as how many *more than* 10 pennies. | Children solve addition facts up to sums of 20. [Operations and Computation Goal 1] |

 **Math Boxes**

Suggestions for using Math Boxes to meet individual needs begin on page 26 of this handbook. There are blank masters for Math Boxes on pages 120–125.

# Using Part 3 of the Lessons

Use your professional judgment, along with assessment results, to determine whether the whole class, small groups, or individual children might benefit from these Unit 4 activities. Consider using the Part 3 Planning Master found on page 138 of this handbook to record your plans.

## Readiness Activities

| Lesson | Activity | Purpose of Activity |
|---|---|---|
| 4♦1 | Fill in missing numbers on thermometer sections. | Gain experience reading the intervals on a thermometer scale. [Measurement and Reference Frames Goal 3] |
| 4♦2 | Compare the lengths of objects. | Explore linear measurements. [Measurement and Reference Frames Goal 1] |
| 4♦3 | Measure length with nonstandard units. | Explore the concept of length. [Measurement and Reference Frames Goal 1] |
| 4♦4 | Compare the lengths of strips of paper by measuring them with cubes. | Explore estimating and comparing lengths. [Measurement and Reference Frames Goal 1] |
| 4♦5 | Write first names using only straight lines. | Gain experience drawing straight lines. [Measurement and Reference Frames Goal 1] |
| 4♦6 | Measure around objects with a string. | Explore measuring non-linear distances. [Measurement and Reference Frames Goal 1] |
| 4♦8 | Set tool-kit clocks to hour and half-hour times. | Gain experience telling time. [Measurement and Reference Frames Goal 4] |
| 4♦9 | Sequence before-school activities. | Explore the concept of time. [Measurement and Reference Frames Goal 4] |
| 4♦10 | Name numbers before and after 2-digit numbers. | Gain experience ordering numbers. [Number and Numeration Goal 7] |
| 4♦11 | Sort dominoes by the total number of dots. | Gain experience with addition problems. [Operations and Computation Goal 2] |
| 4♦12 | Record easy addition facts on index cards. | Gain experience with math facts. [Operations and Computation Goal 1] |

## English Language Learners Support Activities

| Lesson | Activity | Purpose of Activity |
|---|---|---|
| 4♦1 | Add *temperature* to the Math Word Bank. | Make connections among and use visuals to represent terms. [Measurement and Reference Frames Goal 3] |
| 4♦3 | Add *foot* to the Math Word Bank. | Make connections among and use visuals to represent terms. [Measurement and Reference Frames Goal 1] |
| 4♦4 | Add *inch* to the Math Word Bank. | Make connections among and use visuals to represent terms. [Measurement and Reference Frames Goal 1] |
| 4♦8 | Label the classroom clock with *o'clock, quarter-past, quarter-after, half-past, quarter-to,* and *quarter-before.* | Create a language-rich environment. [Measurement and Reference Frames Goal 4] |
| 4♦11 | Add *sum* to the Math Word Bank. | Make connections among and use visuals to represent terms. [Operations and Computation Goal 2] |

# Enrichment Activities

| Lesson | Activity | Purpose of Activity |
|---|---|---|
| 4◆1 | Compare temperature and weather in different cities. | Apply understanding of weather and temperature concepts. [Measurement and Reference Frames Goal 3] |
| 4◆3 | Read and discuss *How Big Is a Foot?* | Apply understanding of standard measurement. [Measurement and Reference Frames Goal 1] |
| 4◆4 | Measure objects between 1 and 2 feet long to the nearest inch. | Apply understanding of linear measurement. [Measurement and Reference Frames Goal 1] |
| 4◆5 | Measure height of bean plants grown in class. | Explore measurement. [Measurement and Reference Frames Goal 1] |
| 4◆6 | Match measuring tools to objects they measure. | Apply understanding of measurement. [Measurement and Reference Frames Goal 1] |
| 4◆7 | Estimate and measure lengths of shapes on geoboards. | Apply estimation skills with linear measurement. [Measurement and Reference Frames Goal 1] |
| 4◆8 | Illustrate activities that can be done in given amounts of time. | Apply understanding of time. [Measurement and Reference Frames Goal 4] |
| 4◆9 | Make a timeline for events in a story. | Explore timelines. [Measurement and Reference Frames Goal 4] |
| 4◆10 | Construct a number-grid poster with stick-on notes. | Explore number-grid patterns. [Patterns, Functions, and Algebra Goal 1] |
| 4◆12 | Find cumulative sums of dice rolls. | Apply understanding of addition. [Operations and Computation Goal 2] |

# Extra Practice Activities

| Lesson | Activity | Purpose of Activity |
|---|---|---|
| 4◆2 | Select measuring tools in *Minute Math+* activities. | Explore measuring. [Measurement and Reference Frames Goal 1] |
| 4◆7 | Describe and identify shapes in *Minute Math+* activities. | Practice with shapes. [Geometry Goal 1] |
| 4◆9 | Sequence dates, days, and months in *Minute Math+* activities. | Practice with the calendar. [Measurement and Reference Frames Goal 4] |
| 4◆11 | Find sums of easy addition facts. | Practice math facts. [Operations and Computation Goal 1] |

*Everyday Mathematics* develops concepts and skills over time. Below is a chart showing where the Grade-Level Goals emphasized in this unit are addressed throughout the year. Use the chart to help you determine which Maintaining Concepts and Skills activities on page 77 to utilize to ensure that children continue working toward these Grade-Level Goals.

- ● Grade-Level Goal is taught.
- ◐ Grade-Level Goal is practiced.
- ○ Grade-Level Goal is not a focus.

| Grade-Level Goals Emphasized in Unit 4 | Unit | | | | | | | | | |
|---|---|---|---|---|---|---|---|---|---|---|
| | 1 | 2 | 3 | 4 | 5 | 6 | 7 | 8 | 9 | 10 |
| **[Number and Numeration Goal 1]** Count on by 1s, 2s, 5s, and 10s past 100 and back by 1s from any number less than 100 with and without number grids, number lines, and calculators. | ● | ● | ● | ● | ● | ● | ◐ | ◐ | ● | ● |
| **[Number and Numeration Goal 7]** Compare and order whole numbers up to 1,000. | ● | ● | ● | ● | ● | ● | ◐ | ◐ | ● | ◐ |
| **[Operations and Computation Goal 1]** Demonstrate proficiency with +/− 0, +/− 1, doubles, and sum-equals-ten addition and subtraction facts such as 6 + 4 = 10 and 10 − 7 = 3. | ● | ◐ | ◐ | ● | ● | ● | ● | ◐ | ◐ | ● |
| **[Operations and Computation Goal 2]** Use manipulatives, number grids, tally marks, mental arithmetic, and calculators to solve problems involving the addition and subtraction of 1-digit whole numbers with 1- or 2-digit whole numbers; calculate and compare the values of combinations of coins. | ● | ● | ● | ● | ● | ● | ● | ● | ● | ● |
| **[Measurement and Reference Frames Goal 1]** Use nonstandard tools and techniques to estimate and compare weight and length; measure length with standard measuring tools. | ○ | ○ | ● | ● | ◐ | ◐ | ○ | ○ | ○ | ◐ |
| **[Measurement and Reference Frames Goal 4]** Use a calendar to identify days, weeks, months, and dates; tell and show time to the nearest half and quarter hour on an analog clock. | ○ | ● | ● | ● | ● | ○ | ◐ | ○ | ◐ | ◐ |

# Maintaining Concepts and Skills

All of the goals addressed in this unit will be addressed again in later units. Here are several suggestions for maintaining concepts and skills until they are formally revisited.

### Number and Numeration Goal 7

◆ Have children play *Top-It*.

◆ Have children sort dominoes according to the total number of dots.

◆ Have children name numbers before and after 2-digit numbers. See the Readiness activity in Lesson 4-10 for more information.

### Operations and Computation Goal 2

◆ Have children play *Domino Top-It* and *Shaker Addition Top-It*.

◆ Use Frames-and-Arrows masters A and B on pages 128 and 129 of this handbook to create practice problems with addition rules.

### Measurement and Reference Frames Goal 1

◆ Have children measure around objects with a string. See the Readiness activity in Lesson 4-6 for more information.

◆ Have children compare the lengths of objects to their copy of the standard foot or to a foot-long ruler.

### Measurement and Reference Frames Goal 4

◆ Have children play *Time Match*.

◆ Show a time on a demonstration clock and have children record this time at the top of their papers before completing assignments.

# Assessment

See page 78 in the *Assessment Handbook* for modifications to the written portion of the Unit 4 Progress Check.

Additionally, see pages 79–83 for modifications to the open-response task and selected child work samples.

# Activities and Ideas for Differentiation

In this unit children continue their work with place value, number stories, and fact power. This section summarizes opportunities for supporting multiple learning styles and ability levels. Use these suggestions to develop a differentiation plan for Unit 5.

## Part 1 Activities That Support Differentiation

Below are examples of Unit 5 activities that highlight some of the general instructional strategies that are hallmarks of a differentiated classroom. These strategies will help you support, emphasize, and enhance lesson content to make sure all your children are engaged in the mathematics at the highest possible level. For more information about general differentiation strategies that accommodate the diverse needs of today's classrooms, see the essay on pages 8–16 of this handbook.

| Lesson | Activity | Strategy |
|--------|----------|----------|
| 5•1 | Children build numbers with base-10 blocks and make exchanges. | Modeling concretely |
| 5•2 | Children perform calculator counts by 1s and 10s. | Modeling physically |
| 5•4 | Children cover a surface with playing cards to calculate the area in cards. | Modeling concretely |
| 5•7 | Children pair up pennies to compare amounts. | Modeling concretely |
| 5•8 | Children draw and complete diagrams to model number stories. | Using organizational tools |
| 5•11 | Children identify patterns in the Facts Table with doubles facts and facts with sums of 10. | Modeling visually |

# Vocabulary Development

The list below identifies the Key Vocabulary terms from this unit. The lesson in which each term is defined is indicated next to the term. Some of these terms or their homophones are used outside of mathematics. Consider adding other words as appropriate for developing understanding of the context of the lessons.

Lessons include suggestions for helping English language learners understand and develop vocabulary. For more information, see pages 17–19 of this handbook.

| Key Vocabulary | | |
|---|---|---|
| *area **5♦4** | function machine **5♦12** | pan balance (*balance) **5♦4** |
| base-10 blocks (*†base) **5♦1** | hundreds **5♦2** | represent **5♦1** |
| cubes **5♦1** | is less than **5♦3** | *rule **5♦12** |
| *difference **5♦7** | is more than (†more) **5♦3** | tens place (†place) **5♦1** |
| *digit **5♦2** | *longs **5♦1** | turn-around fact (†turn) **5♦10** |
| doubles fact **5♦10** | multiple of 10 **5♦9** | |
| *flat **5♦2** | ones place (†place) **5♦1** | |

★ Discuss the everyday and mathematical meanings of the words that are marked with an asterisk.

† For words marked with a dagger, write the words and their homophones on the board. For example, *base* and *bass; more* and *moor; place* and *plaice;* and *turn* and *tern.* Discuss and clarify the meaning of each.

◆ As each word is introduced in the lesson, write the word on the board and discuss its meaning.

◆ List the words on a Math Word Wall for children to see. As each word is introduced in the lesson, add a picture next to the word on the Word Wall.

◆ Use the vocabulary words regularly when teaching lessons, and encourage children to use the words in their discussions.

 **Games**

Below are suggested Unit 5 game adaptations. For more information about implementing games in a differentiated classroom, see pages 20–25 of this handbook.

### Game: *Difference Game*

**Skill Practiced: Solve subtraction facts using only 0–10.** [Operations and Computation Goal 1]

| Modification | Purpose of Modification |
|---|---|
| Players compare each of their totals to 10 pennies. Each player wins the difference between his or her total and 10 pennies. Place a line of 10 pennies on the playing area so players can compare their pennies to 10 pennies. | Children solve subtraction facts with a minuend of 10. [Operations and Computation Goal 1] |
| Players record number models on a half-sheet of paper for each turn. | Children write number sentences using the symbols +, −, and =. [Patterns, Functions, and Algebra Goal 2] |

### Game: *Digit Game*

**Skill Practiced: Compare 2-digit numbers.** [Number and Numeration Goal 7]

| Modification | Purpose of Modification |
|---|---|
| Players draw one card to start. This will be the number for both players' tens place. They keep it throughout the game and change the ones digits in each round. | Children compare 2-digit numbers with the same digit in the tens place. [Number and Numeration Goal 7] |
| Players draw three or four cards on each turn to make their numbers. | Children compare 3- or 4-digit numbers. [Number and Numeration Goal 7] |

### Game: *Shaker Addition Top-It*

**Skill Practiced: Solve addition facts using only 0–6.** [Operations and Computation Goal 1]

| Modification | Purpose of Modification |
|---|---|
| Players choose one addend to use consistently. They only roll the die one time on each turn to generate a second addend; for example, they may play with 5 as one of the addends for each round. | Children solve addition facts with one consistent addend. [Operations and Computation Goal 1] |
| Players use two 10-sided dice labeled 0–9. | Children solve addition facts using the addends 0–9. [Operations and Computation Goal 1] |

## Math Boxes

Suggestions for using Math Boxes to meet individual needs begin on page 26 of this handbook. There are blank masters for Math Boxes on pages 120–125.

# Using Part 3 of the Lessons

Use your professional judgment, along with assessment results, to determine whether the whole class, small groups, or individual children might benefit from these Unit 5 activities. Consider using the Part 3 Planning Master found on page 138 of this handbook to record your plans.

## Readiness Activities

| Lesson | Activity | Purpose of Activity |
|---|---|---|
| 5◆1 | Identify and write numbers to 99. | Gain experience reading and writing numbers. [Number and Numeration Goal 3] |
| 5◆2 | Build designs with base-10 blocks and calculate the value of the designs. | Explore place-value exchanges with base-10 blocks. [Number and Numeration Goal 3] |
| 5◆3 | Count and compare numbers of cubes. | Gain experience comparing quantities. [Number and Numeration Goal 7] |
| 5◆5 | Model number stories with diagrams. | Explore solving parts-and-total problems. [Operations and Computation Goal 4] |
| 5◆6 | Compare numbers of cubes in cups. | Explore comparing quantities. [Number and Numeration Goal 7] |
| 5◆7 | Find distances between numbers on the number grid. | Gain experience finding the difference between two numbers. [Operations and Computation Goal 2] |
| 5◆8 | Act out number stories with counters. | Explore number stories. [Operations and Computation Goal 4] |
| 5◆10 | Hop on a number line to solve facts when the addends are switched. | Explore the Commutative Property of Addition. [Patterns, Functions, and Algebra Goal 3] |
| 5◆11 | Play *Two-Fisted Penny Addition.* | Gain experience with math facts. [Operations and Computation Goal 1] |
| 5◆12 | Add and subtract on a calculator following specified rules. | Gain experience with rules for function machines. [Patterns, Functions, and Algebra Goal 1] |

## English Language Learners Support Activities

| Lesson | Activity | Purpose of Activity |
|---|---|---|
| 5◆3 | Add *greater than, less than,* and *equal* to the Math Word Bank. | Make connections among and use visuals to represent terms. [Number and Numeration Goal 7] |
| 5◆7 | Add *difference* to the Math Word Bank. | Make connections among and use visuals to represent terms. [Operations and Computation Goal 2] |
| 5◆10 | Learn the gesture for *turn-around facts.* | Create a physical model for the term. [Operations and Computation Goal 1] |
| 5◆12 | Add *rule* to the Math Word Bank. | Make connections among and use visuals to represent terms. [Patterns, Functions, and Algebra Goal 1] |

## Enrichment Activities

| Lesson | Activity | Purpose of Activity |
|---|---|---|
| 5◆1 | Use place-value clues to guess the digits in a mystery number. | Apply understanding of place value. [Number and Numeration Goal 3] |
| 5◆3 | Complete number sentences. | Explore the $<$, $>$, and $=$ symbols. [Patterns, Functions, and Algebra Goal 2] |
| 5◆4 | Compare weights of objects. | Explore the concept of weight. [Measurement and Reference Frames Goal 1] |
| 5◆5 | Play *Animal Weight Top-It*. | Explore comparing quantities. [Number and Numeration Goal 7] |
| 5◆6 | Record number sentences for pan-balance problems. | Apply understanding of relation number sentences. [Patterns, Functions, and Algebra Goal 2] |
| 5◆7 | Compare the value of coin combinations. | Explore the relationships among coin values. [Number and Numeration Goal 7] |
| 5◆8 | Write number stories about science or social studies topics. | Apply understanding of number stories. [Operations and Computation Goal 4] |
| 5◆9 | Collect data on dice rolls. | Explore probability. [Data and Chance Goal 2] |
| 5◆12 | Create "What's My Rule?" problems. | Explore solving "What's My Rule?" problems. [Patterns, Functions, and Algebra Goal 1] |
| 5◆13 | Use the calculator as a function machine. | Apply understanding of function machines. [Patterns, Functions, and Algebra Goal 1] |

## Extra Practice Activities

| Lesson | Activity | Purpose of Activity |
|---|---|---|
| 5◆1 | Read *The Warlord's Beads* and draw base-10 blocks to represent numbers from the story. | Practice with place-value concepts. [Number and Numeration Goal 3] |
| 5◆2 | Solve place-value problems using patterns in *Minute Math+* activities. | Practice identifying numbers based on given place-value information and patterns. [Patterns, Functions, and Algebra Goal 1] |
| 5◆3 | Read *Just Enough Carrots* and write number models. | Practice with relation symbols. [Patterns, Functions, and Algebra Goal 2] |
| 5◆4 | Skip count in *Minute Math+* activities. | Practice counting. [Number and Numeration Goal 1] |
| 5◆9 | Read and discuss *Probability Pistachio*. | Practice with probability concepts. [Data and Chance Goal 3] |
| 5◆10 | Play *Domino Top-It*. | Practice determining sums and comparing quantities. [Number and Numeration Goal 7; Operations and Computation Goal 1] |
| 5◆11 | Solve easy addition facts. | Practice finding sums. [Operations and Computation Goal 1] |
| 5◆13 | Solve "What's My Rule?" problems. | Practice solving "What's My Rule?" problems. [Patterns, Functions, and Algebra Goal 1] |

# Looking at Grade-Level Goals

*Everyday Mathematics* develops concepts and skills over time. Below is a chart showing where the Grade-Level Goals emphasized in this unit are addressed throughout the year. Use the chart to help you determine which Maintaining Concepts and Skills activities on page 84 to utilize to ensure that children continue working toward these Grade-Level Goals.

● Grade-Level Goal is taught.
◐ Grade-Level Goal is practiced.
○ Grade-Level Goal is not a focus.

| Grade-Level Goals Emphasized in Unit 5 | Unit 1 | 2 | 3 | 4 | 5 | 6 | 7 | 8 | 9 | 10 |
|---|---|---|---|---|---|---|---|---|---|---|
| [Number and Numeration Goal 1] Count on by 1s, 2s, 5s, and 10s past 100 and back by 1s from any number less than 100 with and without number grids, number lines, and calculators. | ● | ● | ● | ● | ● | ● | ● | ● | ● | ● |
| [Number and Numeration Goal 2] Count collections of objects accurately and reliably; estimate the number of objects in a collection. | ● | ● | ● | ● | ● | ● | ◐ | ◐ | ● | ◐ |
| [Number and Numeration Goal 3] Read, write, and model with manipulatives whole numbers up to 1,000; identify places in such numbers and the values of the digits in those places. | ● | ● | ● | ○ | ● | ◐ | ○ | ● | ◐ | ◐ |
| [Number and Numeration Goal 6] Use manipulatives, drawings, tally marks, and numerical expressions involving addition and subtraction of 1- or 2-digit numbers to give equivalent names for whole numbers up to 100. | ● | ● | ● | ● | ● | ● | ○ | ◐ | ○ | ○ |
| [Number and Numeration Goal 7] Compare and order whole numbers up to 1,000. | ● | ● | ● | ● | ● | ● | ◐ | ◐ | ● | ◐ |
| [Operations and Computation Goal 2] Use manipulatives, number grids, tally marks, mental arithmetic, and calculators to solve problems involving the addition and subtraction of 1-digit whole numbers with 1- or 2-digit whole numbers; calculate and compare the values of combinations of coins. | ● | ● | ● | ● | ● | ● | ● | ● | ◐ | ● |
| [Operations and Computation Goal 4] Identify change-to-more, change-to-less, comparison, and parts-and-total situations. | ○ | ○ | ○ | ◐ | ● | ○ | ◐ | ◐ | ◐ | ● |
| [Patterns, Functions, and Algebra Goal 1] Extend, describe, and create numeric, visual, and concrete patterns; solve problems involving function machines, "What's My Rule?" tables, and Frames-and-Arrows diagrams. | ● | ◐ | ● | ● | ● | ● | ● | ● | ● | ● |
| [Patterns, Functions, and Algebra Goal 2] Read, write, and explain expressions and number sentences using the symbols +, −, and = and the symbols > and < with cues; solve equations involving addition and subtraction. | ○ | ○ | ○ | ○ | ● | ● | ● | ● | ● | ● |
| [Patterns, Functions, and Algebra Goal 3] Apply the Commutative Property of Addition and the Additive Identity to basic addition fact problems. | ○ | ○ | ○ | ○ | ● | ● | ● | ● | ◐ | ○ |

# Maintaining Concepts and Skills

All of the goals addressed in this unit will be addressed again in later units. Here are several suggestions for maintaining concepts and skills until they are formally revisited.

### Number and Numeration Goal 3

◆ Have children play the *Digit Game* and *Base-10 Exchange Game.*

◆ Have children identify and write numbers to 99. See the Readiness activity in Lesson 5-1 for more information.

### Operations and Computation Goal 4

◆ Have children write addition and subtraction number stories. They can draw and complete diagrams to go with the stories.

◆ Have children model number stories with situation diagrams. See the Readiness activity in Lesson 5-5 for more information.

### Patterns, Functions, and Algebra Goal 1

◆ Have children use rules to add and subtract on a calculator. See the Readiness activity in Lesson 5-12 for more information.

◆ Use the "What's My Rule?" master on page 130 of this handbook to create practice problems.

### Patterns, Functions, and Algebra Goal 2

◆ Have children play *Top-It* and *Addition Top-It* and record number sentences for several rounds.

# Assessment

See page 86 in the *Assessment Handbook* for modifications to the written portion of the Unit 5 Progress Check.

Additionally, see pages 87–91 for modifications to the open-response task and selected child work samples.

# Unit 6 · Activities and Ideas for Differentiation

In this unit, children continue to build their fact power with basic addition and subtraction facts. It also extends their experience with telling time, calculating coin combinations, and making linear measurements. This section summarizes opportunities for supporting multiple learning styles and ability levels. Use these suggestions to develop a differentiation plan for Unit 6.

# Part 1 Activities That Support Differentiation

Below are examples of Unit 6 activities that highlight some of the general instructional strategies that are hallmarks of a differentiated classroom. These strategies will help you support, emphasize, and enhance lesson content to make sure all your children are engaged in the mathematics at the highest possible level. For more information about general differentiation strategies that accommodate the diverse needs of today's classrooms, see the essay on pages 8–16 of this handbook.

| Lesson | Activity | Strategy |
|--------|----------|----------|
| 6◆2 | Model equivalencies on a pan balance. | Modeling concretely |
| 6◆3 | Children write fact families to represent the numbers on dominoes. | Modeling visually |
| 6◆6 | Children line up five pennies to create a visual reference for the length of 10 centimeters. | Using a visual reference |
| 6◆7 | Children make triangles with given characteristics on the geoboard. | Modeling concretely |
| 6◆10 | Model counts by 5 on the demonstration clock. As children count, they can make connections between the numerals on the clock face and how many groups of 5 they have counted. | Modeling visually |
| 6◆12 | Children act out finding the middle number of a data set by lining up in order and repeatedly removing the highest and lowest numbers from the group. | Modeling physically |

# Vocabulary Development

The list below identifies the Key Vocabulary terms from this unit. The lesson in which each term is defined is indicated next to the term. Some of these terms or their homophones are used outside of mathematics. Consider adding other words as appropriate for developing understanding of the context of the lessons.

Lessons include suggestions for helping English language learners understand and develop vocabulary. For more information, see pages 17–19 of this handbook.

| Key Vocabulary | | |
|---|---|---|
| Addition/Subtraction Facts Table **6◆1** | fact family **6◆3** | name-collection box (*box) **6◆2** |
| centimeter **6◆6** | Fact Triangle **6◆4** | *quarter **6◆9** |
| cm **6◆6** | metric system **6◆6** | *range **6◆12** |
| digital clock **6◆10** | middle value **6◆12** | table of contents (*table) **6◆11** |
| equivalent names **6◆2** | *My Reference Book* **6◆11** | |

* Discuss the everyday and mathematical meanings of the words that are marked with an asterisk.

◆ As each word is introduced in the lesson, write the word on the board and discuss its meaning.

◆ List the words on a Math Word Wall for children to see. As each word is introduced in the lesson, add a picture next to the word on the Word Wall.

◆ Use the vocabulary words regularly when teaching lessons, and encourage children to use the words in their discussions.

 # Games

Below are suggested Unit 6 game adaptations. For more information about implementing games in a differentiated classroom, see pages 20–25 of this handbook.

## Game: *Addition Top-It*

**Skill Practiced: Solve addition problems and compare sums.** [Number and Numeration Goal 7; Operations and Computation Goal 2]

| Modification | Purpose of Modification |
|---|---|
| Players keep one addend constant. Players turn over one card during a turn and find the sum of that number and their constant number. | Children solve addition facts with a consistent addend and compare sums. [Number and Numeration Goal 7; Operations and Computation Goal 1] |
| Players draw three cards on a turn. They make a 2-digit number for one addend and use the other card for the second addend. | Children use place value to make the largest sum and compare sums. [Number and Numeration Goals 1 and 7; Operations and Computation Goal 2] |

## Game: *Penny Plate*

**Skill Practiced: Solve addition facts.** [Operations and Computation Goal 1]

| Modification | Purpose of Modification |
|---|---|
| Players draw 10 circles on the plate. They place the pennies in the circles and determine how many pennies are under the plate. | Children solve addition facts for sums of 10. [Operations and Computation Goal 1] |
| Players use 10 dimes instead of 10 pennies and determine the amount of money hidden under the plate. | Children solve addition problems with multiples of 10. [Operations and Computation Goal 2] |

## Game: *Coin Exchange*

**Skill Practiced: Make coin exchanges.** [Measurement and Reference Frames Goal 2]

| Modification | Purpose of Modification |
|---|---|
| Players use 30 pennies and 20 dimes. After children make their exchanges, they compare their coins to see who has more money. | Children make coin exchanges. [Measurement and Reference Frames Goal 2] |
| Players use number cards 1–20 (four each of 1–10 and one each of 11–20). They draw one card and take a combination of coins from the bank equal to the number on the card. At the end of five rounds, children calculate the total value of their coins. | Children make coin exchanges and calculate the value of coin combinations. [Operations and Computation Goal 2; Measurement and Reference Frames Goal 2] |

 # Math Boxes

Suggestions for using Math Boxes to meet individual needs begin on page 26 of this handbook. There are blank masters for Math Boxes on pages 120–125.

# Using Part 3 of the Lessons

Use your professional judgment, along with assessment results, to determine whether the whole class, small groups, or individual children might benefit from these Unit 6 activities. Consider using the Part 3 Planning Master found on page 138 of this handbook to record your plans.

## Readiness Activities

| Lesson | Activity | Purpose of Activity |
|---|---|---|
| 6◆1 | Sort and chart domino sums. | Gain experience with sums. [Patterns, Functions, and Algebra Goal 1] |
| 6◆2 | Use counters and number sentences to find equivalent names for a number. | Explore equivalent names for numbers. [Number and Numeration Goal 6] |
| 6◆3 | Write number sentences to represent domino sums. | Gain experience writing number sentences. [Patterns, Functions, and Algebra Goal 2] |
| 6◆4 | Write fact families for dice rolls. | Gain experience with the Commutative Property of Addition. [Patterns, Functions, and Algebra Goal 3] |
| 6◆7 | Identify even and odd numbers and color even and odd patterns on the number grid. | Explore patterns with even and odd numbers. [Number and Numeration Goal 5] |
| 6◆8 | Find missing *out* numbers in "What's My Rule?" tables using calculators. | Explore the "What's My Rule?" table. [Patterns, Functions, and Algebra Goal 1] |
| 6◆9 | Play *Penny-Nickel-Dime Exchange*. | Gain experience making coin exchanges. [Measurement and Reference Frames Goal 2] |
| 6◆10 | Make circular number lines from 0 to 60. | Explore the number of minutes in an hour. [Measurement and Reference Frames Goal 4] |
| 6◆11 | Sequence number cards. | Explore ordinal numbers. [Number and Numeration Goal 7] |
| 6◆12 | Find the lowest and highest values in a data set. | Gain experience finding the minimum and maximum of a data set. [Data and Chance Goal 2] |

## English Language Learners Support Activities

| Lesson | Activity | Purpose of Activity |
|---|---|---|
| 6◆4 | Make *fact family* houses. | Create visual references. [Operations and Computation Goal 1] |
| 6◆6 | Add *centimeter* to the Math Word Bank. | Make connections among and use visuals to represent terms. [Measurement and Reference Frames Goal 1] |
| 6◆7 | Discuss color and shape words related to pattern blocks, such as *triangle, trapezoid, rhombus, hexagon, yellow, green,* and *red.* | Make connections between terms and visual models. [Geometry Goal 1] |
| 6◆9 | Discuss various meanings for *quarter.* | Clarify the mathematical and everyday uses of the term. [Measurement and Reference Frames Goal 2] |
| 6◆12 | Add *range* to the Math Word Bank. | Make connections among and use visuals to represent terms. [Data and Chance Goal 2] |

# Enrichment Activities

| Lesson | Activity | Purpose of Activity |
|---|---|---|
| 6•1 | Predict and record sums for the results of rolling dice. | Apply understanding of finding sums. [Operations and Computation Goal 2] |
| 6•2 | Complete name-collection boxes. | Apply understanding of equivalent names for numbers. [Number and Numeration Goal 6] |
| 6•4 | Use Fact Triangles to solve extended facts. | Explore fact families. [Patterns, Functions, and Algebra Goal 3] |
| 6•5 | Identify and describe patterns in the Addition/Subtraction Facts Table. | Explore the Addition/Subtraction Facts Table. [Operations and Computation Goal 2] |
| 6•6 | Find objects shorter than, longer than, and the same size as a meter. | Explore metric lengths. [Measurement and Reference Frames Goal 1] |
| 6•7 | Find sums of three randomly generated addends. | Explore solving addition problems. [Operations and Computation Goal 2] |
| 6•8 | Solve Frames-and-Arrows problems in which the first few frames are blank. | Apply understanding of identifying and using rules to complete patterns. [Patterns, Functions, and Algebra Goal 1] |
| 6•9 | Play *Quarter-Dime-Nickel-Penny Grab*. | Apply understanding of counting coin combinations. [Operations and Computation Goal 2] |
| 6•12 | Collect and analyze data from a class survey. | Apply understanding of data sets. [Data and Chance Goal 1] |

# Extra Practice Activities

| Lesson | Activity | Purpose of Activity |
|---|---|---|
| 6•2 | Name equivalents for whole numbers and money amounts in *Minute Math+* activities. | Practice finding equivalent names for numbers. [Number and Numeration Goal 6] |
| 6•3 | Write fact families for dominoes. | Practice with addition and subtraction facts. [Patterns, Functions, and Algebra Goal 3] |
| 6•5 | Play *Penny Plate*. | Practice counting up to find the total amount. [Operations and Computation Goal 2] |
| 6•6 | Estimate lengths of objects in *Minute Math+* activities. | Practice estimating length. [Measurement and Reference Frames Goal 1] |
| 6•9 | Read *Deena's Lucky Penny* and show two ways to make 50¢. | Practice making coin combinations. [Operations and Computation Goal 2] |
| 6•10 | Play *Time Match*. | Practice telling time. [Measurement and Reference Frames Goal 4] |
| 6•11 | Identify digits in numbers using place-value clues in *Minute Math+* activities. | Practice with place value. [Number and Numeration Goal 3] |

# Looking at Grade-Level Goals

*Everyday Mathematics* develops concepts and skills over time. Below is a chart showing where the Grade-Level Goals emphasized in this unit are addressed throughout the year. Use the chart to help you determine which Maintaining Concepts and Skills activities on page 91 to utilize to ensure that children continue working toward these Grade-Level Goals.

● Grade-Level Goal is taught.
◐ Grade-Level Goal is practiced.
○ Grade-Level Goal is not a focus.

| Grade-Level Goals Emphasized in Unit 6 | 1 | 2 | 3 | 4 | 5 | 6 | 7 | 8 | 9 | 10 |
|---|---|---|---|---|---|---|---|---|---|---|
| [Number and Numeration Goal 1] Count on by 1s, 2s, 5s, and 10s past 100 and back by 1s from any number less than 100 with and without number grids, number lines, and calculators. | ● | ● | ● | ● | ● | ● | ◐ | ◐ | ● | ● |
| [Number and Numeration Goal 2] Count collections of objects accurately and reliably; estimate the number of objects in a collection. | ● | ● | ● | ● | ◐ | ● | ● | ◐ | ● | ◐ |
| [Number and Numeration Goal 7] Compare and order whole numbers up to 1,000. | ● | ● | ◐ | ● | ◐ | ● | ● | ● | ● | ● |
| [Operations and Computation Goal 1] Demonstrate proficiency with +/− 0, +/− 1, doubles, and sum-equals-ten addition and subtraction facts such as 6 + 4 = 10 and 10 − 7 = 3. | ◐ | ◐ | ◐ | ● | ● | ● | ◐ | ● | ● | ● |
| [Operations and Computation Goal 2] Use manipulatives, number grids, tally marks, mental arithmetic, and calculators to solve problems involving the addition and subtraction of 1-digit whole numbers with 1- or 2-digit whole numbers; calculate and compare the values of combinations of coins. | ● | ● | ● | ● | ● | ● | ◐ | ● | ● | ● |
| [Data and Chance Goal 1] Collect and organize data to create tally charts, tables, bar graphs, and line plots. | ● | ○ | ○ | ○ | ○ | ● | ◐ | ○ | ○ | ● |
| [Geometry Goal 1] Identify and describe plane and solid figures including circles, triangles, squares, rectangles, spheres, cylinders, rectangular prisms, pyramids, cones, and cubes. | ● | ○ | ○ | ○ | ○ | ● | ◐ | ○ | ○ | ● |
| [Patterns, Functions, and Algebra Goal 1] Extend, describe, and create numeric, visual, and concrete patterns; solve problems involving function machines, "What's My Rule?" tables, and Frames-and-Arrows diagrams. | ● | ● | ● | ● | ● | ● | ◐ | ● | ● | ● |
| [Patterns, Functions, and Algebra Goal 2] Read, write, and explain expressions and number sentences using the symbols +, −, and = and the symbols > and < with cues; solve equations involving addition and subtraction. | ○ | ○ | ○ | ○ | ● | ● | ◐ | ● | ● | ○ |
| [Patterns, Functions, and Algebra Goal 3] Apply the Commutative Property of Addition and the Additive Identity to basic addition fact problems. | ○ | ○ | ○ | ○ | ● | ● | ◐ | ● | ● | ○ |

# Maintaining Concepts and Skills

Many of the goals addressed in this unit will be addressed again in later units. Those goals marked with an asterisk (*) are addressed in future units only as practice and application. Here are several suggestions for maintaining concepts and skills until they are formally revisited.

### Number and Numeration Goal 7*

◆ Have children play *The Digit Game*.

◆ Have children sequence number cards. See the Readiness activity in Lesson 6-11 for more information.

### Operations and Computation Goal 1*

◆ Have children play *Penny Plate*.

### Data and Chance Goal 1*

◆ Take a survey once each week and have children make a tally chart or a bar graph to show the results. Some survey suggestions include favorite pets, snacks, ice cream flavors, colors, books, and movies.

### Patterns, Functions, and Algebra Goal 1

◆ Have children sort and chart domino sums. See the Readiness activity in Lesson 6-1 for more information.

◆ Have children find missing output numbers in "What's My Rule?" tables. See the Readiness activity in Lesson 6-8 for more information.

◆ Use Frames-and-Arrows masters A and B on pages 128 and 129 of this handbook to create practice problems.

### Patterns, Functions, and Algebra Goal 3*

◆ Have children write fact families for dice rolls. See the Readiness activity in Lesson 6-4 for more information.

◆ Have children write fact families to match dominoes.

# Assessment

See page 96 in the *Assessment Handbook* for modifications to the written portion of the Unit 6 Progress Check.

Additionally, see pages 97–101 for modifications to the open-response task and selected child work samples.

ASSESSMENT HANDBOOK

Everyday Mathematics

The University of Chicago School Mathematics Project

Grade 1

# Activities and Ideas for Differentiation

In this unit, children explore the attributes of and compare and contrast 2- and 3-dimensional shapes. This section summarizes opportunities for supporting multiple learning styles and ability levels. Use these suggestions to develop a differentiation plan for Unit 7.

# Part 1 Activities That Support Differentiation

Below are examples of Unit 7 activities that highlight some of the general instructional strategies that are hallmarks of a differentiated classroom. These strategies will help you support, emphasize, and enhance lesson content to make sure all your children are engaged in the mathematics at the highest possible level. For more information about general differentiation strategies that accommodate the diverse needs of today's classrooms, see the essay on pages 8–16 of this handbook.

| Lesson | Activity | Strategy |
|--------|----------|----------|
| 7✦1 | Sort children based on the attribute blocks they have. | Modeling physically |
| 7✦3 | Children trace pattern-block shapes using a pattern-block template. | Modeling physically |
| 7✦4 | Children build shapes out of straws and twist-ties to explore the properties of shapes. | Modeling concretely |
| 7✦5 | Children investigate the properties of shapes with curved surfaces by rolling shapes. | Modeling physically |
| 7✦6 | Children use models of pyramids, cones, and cubes to compare the properties of these shapes. | Using a visual reference |
| 7✦7 | Children make symmetrical shapes by cutting a folded piece of paper. | Modeling concretely |

# Vocabulary Development

The list below identifies the Key Vocabulary terms from this unit. The lesson in which each term is defined is indicated next to the term. Some of these terms or their homophones are used outside of mathematics. Consider adding other words as appropriate for developing understanding of the context of the lessons.

Lessons include suggestions for helping English language learners understand and develop vocabulary. For more information, see pages 17–19 of this handbook.

| Key Vocabulary | | |
|---|---|---|
| attribute 7♦1 | polygon 7♦3 | square corner 7♦3 |
| circle 7♦1 | pyramid 7♦6 | surface 7♦5 |
| cone 7♦6 | rectangle 7♦1 | symmetrical 7♦7 |
| *corner 7♦3 | rectangular prism 7♦5 | symmetry 7♦7 |
| cube 7♦6 | rhombus 7♦3 | trapezoid 7♦3 |
| cylinder 7♦5 | *†side 7♦3 | triangle 7♦1 |
| *face 7♦5 | sphere 7♦5 | |
| hexagon 7♦1 | square 7♦1 | |

* Discuss the everyday and mathematical meanings of the words that are marked with an asterisk.

† For the word marked with a dagger, write *side* and its homophone *sighed* on the board. Discuss and clarify the meaning of each.

◆ As each word is introduced in the lesson, write the word on the board and discuss its meaning.

◆ List the words on a Math Word Wall for children to see. As each word is introduced in the lesson, add a picture next to the word on the Word Wall.

◆ Use the vocabulary words regularly when teaching lessons, and encourage children to use the words in their discussions.

 **Games**

Below are suggested Unit 7 game adaptations. For more information about implementing games in a differentiated classroom, see pages 20–25 of this handbook.

| **Game: *Attribute Train Game*** | |
|---|---|
| **Skill Practiced: Follow a rule.** [Patterns, Functions, and Algebra Goal 1] | |
| **Modification** | **Purpose of Modification** |
| Limit the set of blocks so that players are using blocks of only one thickness or maybe the set has fewer shapes. | Children identify and follow a rule involving one attribute. [Patterns, Functions, and Algebra Goal 1] |
| Players have a set of number cards 1–4, four of each. On each turn, they turn over a number card to determine how many attributes must be different for the next block. | Children identify and follow a rule that may involve from one to four attributes. [Patterns, Functions, and Algebra Goal 1] |

| **Game: *Addition Top-It*** | |
|---|---|
| **Skill Practiced: Solve addition problems and compare sums.** [Number and Numeration Goal 7; Operations and Computation Goal 2] | |
| **Modification** | **Purpose of Modification** |
| Players model their numbers with counters to help them solve problems. | Children solve addition problems using a concrete model and compare sums. [Number and Numeration Goal 7; Operations and Computation Goal 2] |
| Players each get a 0 card to start and on each turn, they draw three more cards to make two 2-digit numbers. (One number should be a multiple of 10.) | Children solve 2-digit addition problems with a multiple of 10 for one addend and compare sums. [Number and Numeration Goal 7; Operations and Computation Goal 2] |

| **Game: *Time Match*** | |
|---|---|
| **Skill Practiced: Match analog and digital clocks.** [Measurement and Reference Frames Goal 4] | |
| **Modification** | **Purpose of Modification** |
| At the end of the game, have players put their clocks in order for a bonus point. | Children match analog and digital clocks and put the clocks in order from earlier to later. [Measurement and Reference Frames Goal 4] |
| Instead of matching clocks, players shuffle all of the cards, draw two, and tell how much time elapses between the two times they have drawn. Use the appropriate range of clocks for the players, for example, only to the hour and half-hour, or all of the cards. | Children tell the time on two clocks and calculate the hours and minutes that elapse between the two times shown on the clocks. [Measurement and Reference Frames Goal 4] |

 **Math Boxes**

Suggestions for using Math Boxes to meet individual needs begin on page 26 of this handbook. There are blank masters for Math Boxes on pages 120–125.

# Using Part 3 of the Lessons

Use your professional judgment, along with assessment results, to determine whether the whole class, small groups, or individual children might benefit from these Unit 7 activities. Consider using the Part 3 Planning Master found on page 138 of this handbook to record your plans.

## Readiness Activities

| Lesson | Activity | Purpose of Activity |
|--------|----------|---------------------|
| 7♦1 | Determine attribute rules for groups of children. | Explore the meaning and use of attributes. [Patterns, Functions, and Algebra Goal 1] |
| 7♦2 | Sort classroom objects by attributes. | Gain experience with attributes. [Patterns, Functions, and Algebra Goal 1] |
| 7♦3 | Take turns drawing and guessing pattern-block shapes. | Gain experience identifying shapes. [Geometry Goal 1] |
| 7♦4 | Cut pictures of 2-dimensional shapes from magazines to match a set of shapes. | Gain experience with polygons. [Geometry Goal 1] |
| 7♦5 | Trace and name faces of 3-dimensional shapes. | Explore the relationships between plane shapes and solid figures. [Geometry Goal 1] |
| 7♦6 | Identify 3-dimensional shapes by touch. | Explore the attributes of solid figures. [Geometry Goal 1] |

## English Language Learners Support Activities

| Lesson | Activity | Purpose of Activity |
|--------|----------|---------------------|
| 7♦1 | Use geometric objects, pictures, and gestures to communicate about geometry. | Make connections among and use visuals to represent terms. [Geometry Goal 1] |
| 7♦3 | Add *side* and *corner* to the Math Word Bank. | Make connections among and use visuals to represent terms. [Geometry Goal 1] |
| 7♦5 | Describe shapes using words such as *side, corner, surface, flat, face, circle, triangle, square, sphere, cylinder,* and *rectangular prism* in the Shapes Museum. | Make connections between mathematics and everyday life; discuss new mathematical ideas. [Geometry Goal 1] |

## Enrichment Activities

| Lesson | Activity | Purpose of Activity |
|---|---|---|
| 7✦1 | Sort attribute blocks based on attributes. | Apply understanding of attributes. [Patterns, Functions, and Algebra Goal 1] |
| 7✦2 | Solve Attribute-Train Puzzles. | Apply understanding of attributes. [Patterns, Functions, and Algebra Goal 1] |
| 7✦3 | Create a pattern-block design. | Explore polygon relationships. [Geometry Goal 1] |
| 7✦4 | Compare polygons and figures that are not polygons using Venn diagrams. | Explore attributes of polygons. [Geometry Goal 1] |
| 7✦5 | Sort 3-dimensional shapes by their faces. | Explore the characteristics of solid figures. [Geometry Goal 1] |
| 7✦6 | Compare and contrast prisms and pyramids using Venn diagrams. | Compare the attributes of solid figures. [Geometry Goal 1] |
| 7✦7 | Use mirrors to complete symmetrical shapes. | Explore the concept of symmetry. [Geometry Goal 2] |

## Extra Practice Activities

| Lesson | Activity | Purpose of Activity |
|---|---|---|
| 7✦2 | Solve addition and subtraction problems. | Practice addition and subtraction. [Operations and Computation Goal 2] |
| 7✦3 | Read *Round Is a Mooncake* and draw squares and rectangles. | Practice geometry skills. [Geometry Goal 1] |
| 7✦6 | Read *Cubes, Cones, and Cylinders* and draw something shaped like a cube. | Practice geometry skills. [Geometry Goal 1] |
| 7✦7 | Play *Make My Design.* | Practice naming and describing geometric figures and spatial relationships. [Geometry Goal 1] |

# Looking at Grade-Level Goals

*Everyday Mathematics* develops concepts and skills over time. Below is a chart showing where the Grade-Level Goals emphasized in this unit are addressed throughout the year. Use the chart to help you determine which Maintaining Concepts and Skills activities on page 98 to utilize to ensure that children continue working toward these Grade-Level Goals.

- ● Grade-Level Goal is taught.
- ◐ Grade-Level Goal is practiced.
- ○ Grade-Level Goal is not a focus.

| Grade-Level Goals Emphasized in Unit 7 | 1 | 2 | 3 | 4 | 5 | 6 | 7 | 8 | 9 | 10 |
|---|---|---|---|---|---|---|---|---|---|---|
| [Number and Numeration Goal 2] Count collections of objects accurately and reliably; estimate the number of objects in a collection. | ● | ● | ● | ● | ● | ● | ● | ● | ◐ | ◐ |
| [Geometry Goal 1] Identify and describe plane and solid figures including circles, triangles, squares, rectangles, spheres, cylinders, rectangular prisms, pyramids, cones, and cubes. | ● | ○ | ○ | ○ | ○ | ● | ● | ◐ | ◐ | ◐ |
| [Geometry Goal 2] Identify shapes having line symmetry; complete line-symmetric shapes or designs. | ○ | ○ | ○ | ○ | ○ | ● | ● | ● | ● | ○ |
| [Patterns, Functions, and Algebra Goal 1] Extend, describe, and create numeric, visual, and concrete patterns; solve problems involving function machines, "What's My Rule?" tables, and Frames-and-Arrows diagrams. | ● | ● | ◐ | ◐ | ● | ● | ● | ◐ | ● | ◐ |
| [Patterns, Functions, and Algebra Goal 2] Read, write, and explain expressions and number sentences using the symbols $+$, $-$, and $=$ and the symbols $>$ and $<$ with cues; solve equations involving addition and subtraction. | ○ | ● | ● | ○ | ● | ● | ● | ● | ● | ● |

# Maintaining Concepts and Skills

Many of the goals addressed in this unit will be addressed again in later units. Those goals marked with an asterisk (*) are addressed in future units only as practice and application. Here are several suggestions for maintaining concepts and skills until they are formally revisited.

## Geometry Goal 1*

◆ Have children cut out pictures of 2-dimensional shapes from magazines and make posters using their cut-out shapes. See the Readiness activity in Lesson 7-4 for more information.

◆ Have children trace and name faces of 3-dimensional shapes. See the Readiness activity in Lesson 7-5 for more information.

## Geometry Goal 2*

◆ Have children build a pattern-block design. Then have children build its mirror image across a line of reflection so they have a symmetric design.

## Patterns, Functions, and Algebra Goal 1

◆ Have children play the *Attribute Train Game*.

◆ Have children determine attribute rules given clues. See the Readiness activity in Lesson 7-1 for more information.

◆ Use the "What's My Rule?" master on page 130 of this handbook and Frames-and-Arrows masters A and B on pages 128 and 129 of this handbook to create practice problems.

## Patterns, Functions, and Algebra Goal 2

◆ Have children play *Addition Top-It* and record number sentences for their addition problems.

# Assessment

See page 104 in the *Assessment Handbook* for modifications to the written portion of the Unit 7 Progress Check.

Additionally, see pages 105–109 for modifications to the open-response task and selected child work samples.

# Activities and Ideas for Differentiation

In this unit, children build on their previous experience with money and place value, and they begin to more formally explore fraction concepts. This section summarizes opportunities for supporting multiple learning styles and ability levels. Use these suggestions to develop a differentiation plan for Unit 8.

## Part 1 Activities That Support Differentiation

Below are examples of Unit 8 activities that highlight some of the general instructional strategies that are hallmarks of a differentiated classroom. These strategies will help you support, emphasize, and enhance lesson content to make sure all your children are engaged in the mathematics at the highest possible level. For more information about general differentiation strategies that accommodate the diverse needs of today's classrooms, see the essay on pages 8–16 of this handbook.

| Lesson | Activity | Strategy |
|---|---|---|
| 8◆2 | Children exchange coins on a place-value mat to explore coin equivalencies. | Using organizational tools |
| 8◆3 | Children represent 2-digit numbers using base-10 blocks. | Modeling concretely |
| 8◆4 | Children explore number stories involving money in the context of shopping. | Connecting to everyday life |
| 8◆6 | Children identify objects in the classroom that are broken into some number of equal parts. | Connecting to everyday life |
| 8◆7 | Children fold a piece of paper into quarters (or fourths), label each section as $\frac{1}{4}$, and color each section with a different color to build fraction sense for quarters. | Modeling physically |
| 8◆8 | Children share pennies equally with some number of friends to explore division. | Modeling concretely |

# Vocabulary Development

The list below identifies the Key Vocabulary terms from this unit. The lesson in which each term is defined is indicated next to the term. Some of these terms or their homophones are used outside of mathematics. Consider adding other words as appropriate for developing understanding of the context of the lessons.

Lessons include suggestions for helping English language learners understand and develop vocabulary. For more information, see pages 17–19 of this handbook.

## Key Vocabulary

| | | |
|---|---|---|
| decimal point (*point) **8◆2** | hundreds **8◆3** | tens place (†place) **8◆3** |
| equal parts **8◆6** | hundreds place **8◆3** | thirds **8◆6** |
| fourths **8◆6** | near doubles **8◆9** | to make change (*change) **8◆5** |
| fraction **8◆7** | ones **8◆3** | †whole **8◆6** |
| fractional part **8◆7** | ones place **8◆3** | |
| halves **8◆6** | tens **8◆3** | |

\*  Discuss the everyday and mathematical meanings of the words that are marked with an asterisk.

†  For words marked with a dagger, write the words and their homophones on the board. For example, *place* and *plaice* and *whole* and *hole*. Discuss and clarify the meaning of each.

◆  As each word is introduced in the lesson, write the word on the board and discuss its meaning.

◆  List the words on a Math Word Wall for children to see. As each word is introduced in the lesson, add a picture next to the word on the Word Wall.

◆  Use the vocabulary words regularly when teaching lessons, and encourage children to use the words in their discussions.

 # Games

Below are suggested Unit 8 game adaptations. For more information about implementing games in a differentiated classroom, see pages 20–25 of this handbook.

## Game: *Coin Top-It*

**Skill Practiced: Calculate and compare values of coin combinations.** [Operations and Computation Goal 2]

| Modification | Purpose of Modification |
|---|---|
| Players make a set of coin cards by labeling the coins with their values instead of P, N, D, Q. They get a bonus point if they make a combination to model the total on the card. | Children calculate and compare values of coin combinations. [Operations and Computation Goal 2] |
| Players make a set of cards in which each card has four to six coins on it. They record a number sentence they can use to find the total value of the coin combination. | Children calculate and compare values of coin combinations and record number sentences to represent coin combinations. [Operations and Computation Goal 2; Patterns, Functions, and Algebra Goal 2] |

## Game: *3, 2, 1 Game*

**Skill Practiced: Solve subtraction problems.** [Operations and Computation Goal 2]

| Modification | Purpose of Modification |
|---|---|
| Players begin with 15 instead of 21. They use 15 counters and play the game by physically removing counters each time. | Children solve subtraction problems with minuends of 15 or less. [Operations and Computation Goal 2] |
| Players record a pattern they found that might help someone win the game. For example, "I know that if your partner gets 4, then you can win." | Children identify a pattern in playing the *3, 2, 1, Game*. [Patterns, Functions, and Algebra Goal 1] |

## Game: *Tric-Trac*

**Skill Practiced: Solve addition problems.** [Operations and Computation Goal 2]

| Modification | Purpose of Modification |
|---|---|
| Change the *Tric-Trac* game board to include two 1s, 2s, 3s, 4s, and 5s instead of one of each number 0–9. Players roll only 1 die. | Children solve addition problems with addends less than 6. [Operations and Computation Goal 2] |
| Players record number sentences to show what they did on each turn. | Children solve addition problems and record number models. [Operations and Computation Goal 2; Patterns, Functions, and Algebra Goal 2] |

 # Math Boxes

Suggestions for using Math Boxes to meet individual needs begin on page 26 of this handbook. There are blank masters for Math Boxes on pages 120–125.

# Using Part 3 of the Lessons

Use your professional judgment, along with assessment results, to determine whether the whole class, small groups, or individual children might benefit from these Unit 8 activities. Consider using the Part 3 Planning Master found on page 138 of this handbook to record your plans.

## Readiness Activities

| Lesson | Activity | Purpose of Activity |
|---|---|---|
| 8◆1 | Find the values of groups of coins by skip counting on a calculator. | Gain experience counting coin combinations. [Operations and Computation Goal 2] |
| 8◆2 | Make and record coin exchanges. | Explore the relationships among the values of coins. [Measurement and Reference Frames Goal 2] |
| 8◆3 | Count base-10 blocks by skip counting on a calculator. | Explore place-value concepts. [Number and Numeration Goal 3] |
| 8◆4 | Use counters and situation diagrams to model number stories. | Explore number stories. [Operations and Computation Goal 4] |
| 8◆5 | Play the *Difference Game.* | Explore counting up as a strategy for solving addition and subtraction problems. [Operations and Computation Goal 2] |
| 8◆7 | Fold paper shapes into halves. | Explore dividing shapes into equal parts. [Number and Numeration Goal 4] |
| 8◆9 | Fold paper shapes in half to test for symmetry. | Explore the concept of symmetry. [Geometry Goal 2] |

## English Language Learners Support Activities

| Lesson | Activity | Purpose of Activity |
|---|---|---|
| 8◆2 | Examine *dollar bills.* | Make connections among and use visuals to represent terms. [Measurement and Reference Frames Goal 2] |
| 8◆6 | Add *whole* and *one half* to the Math Word Bank. | Make connections among and use visuals to represent terms. [Number and Numeration Goal 4] |
| 8◆8 | Add *equal parts* and *fraction* to the Math Word Bank. | Make connections among and use visuals to represent terms. [Number and Numeration Goal 4] |

# Enrichment Activities

| Lesson | Activity | Purpose of Activity |
|--------|----------|---------------------|
| 8◆1 | Write and solve coin riddles. | Apply knowledge of counting coin combinations. [Operations and Computation Goal 2] |
| 8◆2 | Show coin combinations that total one dollar. | Explore the value of a dollar. [Measurement and Reference Frames Goal 2] |
| 8◆3 | Play a variation of the *Digit Game* with 3-digit numbers. | Apply understanding of place-value concepts. [Number and Numeration Goal 3] |
| 8◆4 | Make a shopping list with items totaling ten dollars. | Apply understanding of money concepts. [Operations and Computation Goal 2] |
| 8◆5 | Count up to one dollar to make change. | Apply understanding of making change. [Operations and Computation Goal 2] |
| 8◆6 | Divide cereal into equal portions. | Explore the concept of sharing a quantity equally. [Number and Numeration Goal 4] |
| 8◆7 | Make fraction books of objects divided into equal parts. | Apply understanding of fraction concepts. [Number and Numeration Goal 4] |
| 8◆8 | Make fraction creatures from different-colored squares of paper. | Apply understanding of fractions of a set. [Number and Numeration Goal 4] |

# Extra Practice Activities

| Lesson | Activity | Purpose of Activity |
|--------|----------|---------------------|
| 8◆1 | Play *Coin Top-It*. | Practice comparing money amounts. [Operations and Computation Goal 2] |
| 8◆2 | Find multiples of money amounts in *Minute Math+* activities. | Practice finding money amounts. [Operations and Computation Goal 2] |
| 8◆3 | Order numbers represented with base-10 blocks. | Practice with place value. [Number and Numeration Goal 3] |
| 8◆8 | Find the number of parts in a whole in *Minute Math+* activities. | Practice with fractions. [Number and Numeration Goal 4] |
| 8◆9 | Play *Two-Fisted Penny Addition* with 17 and 18 pennies. | Practice finding complements for sums. [Operations and Computation Goal 2] |

# Looking at Grade-Level Goals

*Everyday Mathematics* develops concepts and skills over time. Below is a chart showing where the Grade-Level Goals emphasized in this unit are addressed throughout the year. Use the chart to help you determine which Maintaining Concepts and Skills activities on page 105 to utilize to ensure that children continue working toward these Grade-Level Goals.

- ● Grade-Level Goal is taught.
- ◐ Grade-Level Goal is practiced.
- ○ Grade-Level Goal is not a focus.

| Grade-Level Goals Emphasized in Unit 8 | Unit 1 | 2 | 3 | 4 | 5 | 6 | 7 | 8 | 9 | 10 |
|---|---|---|---|---|---|---|---|---|---|---|
| [Number and Numeration Goal 2] Count collections of objects accurately and reliably; estimate the number of objects in a collection. | ● | ● | ● | ◐ | ● | ● | ● | ● | ◐ | ◐ |
| [Number and Numeration Goal 3] Read, write, and model with manipulatives whole numbers up to 1,000; identify places in such numbers and the values of the digits in those places. | ● | ● | ● | ○ | ◐ | ◐ | ○ | ● | ◐ | ◐ |
| [Number and Numeration Goal 4] Use manipulatives and drawings to model halves, thirds, and fourths as equal parts of a region or a collection; describe the model. | ○ | ○ | ○ | ○ | ○ | ○ | ◐ | ◐ | ● | ◐ |
| [Operations and Computation Goal 2] Use manipulatives, number grids, tally marks, mental arithmetic, and calculators to solve problems involving the addition and subtraction of 1-digit whole numbers with 1- or 2-digit whole numbers; calculate and compare the values of combinations of coins. | ● | ● | ● | ● | ● | ● | ● | ● | ● | ● |
| [Operations and Computation Goal 4] Identify change-to-more, change-to-less, comparison, and parts-and-total situations. | ○ | ○ | ○ | ◐ | ◐ | ○ | ◐ | ● | ● | ◐ |
| [Measurement and Reference Frames Goal 2] Know and compare the value of pennies, nickels, dimes, quarters, and dollar bills; make exchanges between coins. | ○ | ● | ● | ◐ | ● | ● | ◐ | ● | ● | ● |
| [Patterns, Functions, and Algebra Goal 2] Read, write, and explain expressions and number sentences using the symbols +, −, and = and the symbols > and < with cues; solve equations involving addition and subtraction. | ○ | ● | ● | ○ | ◐ | ◐ | ● | ● | ● | ● |

# Maintaining Concepts and Skills

Many of the goals addressed in this unit will be addressed again in later units. Those goals marked with an asterisk (*) are addressed in future units only as practice and application. Here are several suggestions for maintaining concepts and skills until they are formally revisited.

### Number and Numeration Goal 2*

◆ Have children play *Penny Grab* with varying amounts of pennies, for example, 30 pennies.

### Number and Numeration Goal 3*

◆ Have children play *Base-10 Exchange*.

◆ Have children count base-10 blocks by skip counting on a calculator. See the Readiness activity in Lesson 8-3 for more information.

### Operations and Computation Goal 4

◆ Have children use dominoes to model parts-and-total situations, play *Penny Grab* to model comparison situations, and play *Before and After* to model change situations.

◆ Have children use counters and situation diagrams to model number stories. See the Readiness activity in Lesson 8-4 for more information.

◆ Have children write number stories and use the Situation Diagrams for Number Stories master on page 135 of this handbook to complete situation diagrams for the number stories.

### Measurement and Reference Frames Goal 2*

◆ Have children play *Coin Exchange*.

◆ Have children show different coin combinations for the same amount. See the Readiness activity in Lesson 8-2 for more information.

## Assessment

See page 112 in the *Assessment Handbook* for modifications to the written portion of the Unit 8 Progress Check.

Additionally, see pages 113–117 for modifications to the open-response task and selected child work samples.

# Activities and Ideas for Differentiation

In this unit, children explore adding and subtracting with multiples of ten, and continue to develop fraction concepts. This section summarizes opportunities for supporting multiple learning styles and ability levels. Use these suggestions to develop a differentiation plan for Unit 9.

## Part 1 Activities That Support Differentiation

Below are examples of Unit 9 activities that highlight some of the general instructional strategies that are hallmarks of a differentiated classroom. These strategies will help you support, emphasize, and enhance lesson content to make sure all your children are engaged in the mathematics at the highest possible level. For more information about general differentiation strategies that accommodate the diverse needs of today's classrooms, see the essay on pages 8–16 of this handbook.

| Lesson | Activity | Strategy |
|---|---|---|
| 9◆1 | Children use patterns on the number grid to identify hidden numbers. | Modeling visually |
| 9◆4 | Children use number-grid patterns or counting on the number grid to solve addition and subtraction number stories. | Modeling visually |
| 9◆5 | Children explore capacity by filling different containers with popcorn. | Modeling concretely |
| 9◆5 | Children use pattern blocks to build designs reflected across a line of symmetry. | Modeling concretely |
| 9◆6 | Children fold squares into halves in different ways to explore the concept of $\frac{1}{2}$. | Modeling physically |
| 9◆8 | Children use fraction strips to compare fractions. | Using a visual reference |

# Vocabulary Development

The list below identifies the Key Vocabulary terms from this unit. The lesson in which each term is defined is indicated next to the term. Some of these terms or their homophones are used outside of mathematics. Consider adding other words as appropriate for developing understanding of the context of the lessons.

Lessons include suggestions for helping English language learners understand and develop vocabulary. For more information, see pages 17–19 of this handbook.

| Key Vocabulary |
| --- |
| denominator 9◆7 |
| number-grid puzzle 9◆3 |
| numerator 9◆7 |

◆ As each word is introduced in the lesson, write the word on the board and discuss its meaning.

◆ List the words on a Math Word Wall for children to see. As each word is introduced in the lesson, add a picture next to the word on the Word Wall.

◆ Use the vocabulary words regularly when teaching lessons, and encourage children to use the words in their discussions.

 **Games**

Below are suggested Unit 9 game adaptations. For more information about implementing games in a differentiated classroom, see pages 20–25 of this handbook.

| Game: *Beat the Calculator* | |
| --- | --- |
| **Skill Practiced: Solve addition problems.** [Operations and Computation Goal 2] | |
| **Modification** | **Purpose of Modification** |
| One addend remains constant throughout the game and the caller draws only one card for each turn. For example, every addition fact will involve "+1." | Children solve addition problems in which one of the addends is always the same. [Operations and Computation Goal 2] |
| The caller draws a triangle from the set of Fact Triangles. and gives either an addition or a subtraction fact. | Children solve addition and subtraction problems. [Operations and Computation Goal 2] |

| Game: *Number-Grid Game* | |
| --- | --- |
| **Skill Practiced: Solve addition problems on the number grid.** [Operations and Computation Goal 2] | |
| **Modification** | **Purpose of Modification** |
| Players use exactly the number showing on the die (not 10 or 20) and play to a total of 50 instead of 110. | Children solve addition problems on the number grid adding from 0–6 on each turn. [Operations and Computation Goal 2] |
| Add a second die to the game that has + on four sides and − on two sides. Players roll both a number cube and the new die on each turn and move forward or backward the number of steps indicated. | Children add and subtract on the number grid and solve change-to-more and change-to-less problems. [Operations and Computation Goal 2; Operations and Computation Goal 4] |

| Game: *One Dollar Exchange Game* | |
| --- | --- |
| **Skill Practiced: Exchanging coins and bills.** [Measurement and Reference Frames Goal 2] | |
| **Modification** | **Purpose of Modification** |
| Players use a bank of 30 dimes and three dollars. They roll one die on each turn and collect that number of dimes. The first player to get two dollars wins. | Children exchange dimes for dollars. [Measurement and Reference Frames Goal 2] |
| Increase the bank to 10 dollar bills. Players use number cards 1–20 (four each of 1–10 and one each of 11–20). On each turn, players take a combination of pennies and dimes for the total value on the card. The winner is the first player to collect five dollar bills. | Children exchange pennies, dimes, and dollar bills. [Measurement and Reference Frames Goal 2] |

 **Math Boxes**

Suggestions for using Math Boxes to meet individual needs begin on page 26 of this handbook. There are blank masters for Math Boxes on pages 120–125.

# Using Part 3 of the Lessons

Use your professional judgment, along with assessment results, to determine whether the whole class, small groups, or individual children might benefit from these Unit 9 activities. Consider using the Part 3 Planning Master found on page 138 of this handbook to record your plans.

## Readiness Activities

| Lesson | Activity | Purpose of Activity |
|--------|----------|---------------------|
| 9◆1 | Assemble a number grid from number-grid puzzle pieces. | Explore number-grid patterns. [Patterns, Functions, and Algebra Goal 1] |
| 9◆2 | Model numbers using base-10 blocks counting backward and forward by 10s. | Explore counting patterns in digits. [Patterns, Functions, and Algebra Goal 1] |
| 9◆3 | Play *Pin the Number on the Number Grid.* | Explore using patterns in the number grid to find missing numbers. [Patterns, Functions, and Algebra Goal 1] |
| 9◆4 | Use base-10 blocks to solve 2-digit addition and subtraction problems. | Explore adding and subtracting 2-digit numbers. [Operations and Computation Goal 2] |
| 9◆5 | Make symmetric pictures with paint. | Explore the concept of symmetry. [Geometry Goal 2] |
| 9◆6 | Divide 2-dimensional shapes into equal parts and label the parts with their fraction names. | Explore finding fractional parts of a region. [Number and Numeration Goal 4] |
| 9◆7 | Match fractions to circles divided into fractional parts. | Gain experience identifying fractions. [Number and Numeration Goal 4] |

## English Language Learners Support Activities

| Lesson | Activity | Purpose of Activity |
|--------|----------|---------------------|
| 9◆4 | Weigh objects and compare their weights. | Make connections between new terms and everyday experiences. [Measurement and Reference Frames Goal 1] |
| 9◆5 | Add *measurement* and *capacity* to the Math Word Bank. | Make connections among and use visuals to represent terms. [Measurement and Reference Frames Goal 1] |
| 9◆6 | Draw pictures representing unit fractions. | Create visual references for new terms. [Number and Numeration Goal 4] |

# Enrichment Activities

| Lesson | Activity | Purpose of Activity |
|---|---|---|
| 9◆2 | Develop a shortcut for subtraction using patterns on the number grid. | Explore using number-grid patterns to solve problems. [Patterns, Functions, and Algebra Goal 1] |
| 9◆3 | Solve arrow-path problems. | Apply understanding of patterns on the number grid. [Patterns, Functions, and Algebra Goal 1] |
| 9◆4 | Play a variation of *Addition Top-It* using animal-length cards. | Explore 2-digit by 2-digit addition. [Operations and Computation Goal 2] |
| 9◆5 | Estimate how much containers hold. | Explore capacity. [Measurement and Reference Frames Goal 1] |
| 9◆7 | Compare fractions. | Apply understanding of fractions. [Number and Numeration Goal 4] |
| 9◆8 | Find fraction combinations equivalent to $\frac{1}{2}$ and to 1. | Explore equivalent fractions. [Number and Numeration Goal 4] |

# Extra Practice Activities

| Lesson | Activity | Purpose of Activity |
|---|---|---|
| 9◆1 | Fill in number scrolls for larger numbers. | Practice completing a number grid using patterns. [Patterns, Functions, and Algebra Goal 1] |
| 9◆2 | Solve addition and subtraction problems with multiples of 10 in *Minute Math+* activities. | Practice solving addition and subtraction problems. [Operations and Computation Goal 2] |
| 9◆5 | Create symmetrical shapes on a geoboard. | Practice with symmetry. [Geometry Goal 2] |
| 9◆8 | Complete name-collection boxes for fractions. | Practice finding equivalent names for fractions. [Number and Numeration Goal 4] |

# Looking at Grade-Level Goals

*Everyday Mathematics* develops concepts and skills over time. Below is a chart showing where the Grade-Level Goals emphasized in this unit are addressed throughout the year. Use the chart to help you determine which Maintaining Concepts and Skills activities on page 112 to utilize to ensure that children continue working toward these Grade-Level Goals.

- ● Grade-Level Goal is taught.
- ◐ Grade-Level Goal is practiced.
- ○ Grade-Level Goal is not a focus.

| Grade-Level Goals Emphasized in Unit 9 | 1 | 2 | 3 | 4 | 5 | 6 | 7 | 8 | 9 | 10 |
|---|---|---|---|---|---|---|---|---|---|---|
| [**Number and Numeration Goal 1**] Count on by 1s, 2s, 5s, and 10s past 100 and back by 1s from any number less than 100 with and without number grids, number lines, and calculators. | ● | ● | ● | ● | ● | ● | ◐ | ◐ | ● | ● |
| [**Number and Numeration Goal 4**] Use manipulatives and drawings to model halves, thirds, and fourths as equal parts of a region or a collection; describe the model. | ○ | ○ | ○ | ○ | ○ | ○ | ● | ● | ● | ◐ |
| [**Operations and Computation Goal 2**] Use manipulatives, number grids, tally marks, mental arithmetic, and calculators to solve problems involving the addition and subtraction of 1-digit whole numbers with 1- or 2-digit whole numbers; calculate and compare the values of combinations of coins. | ● | ● | ● | ● | ● | ● | ● | ● | ● | ● |
| [**Patterns, Functions, and Algebra Goal 1**] Extend, describe, and create numeric, visual, and concrete patterns; solve problems involving function machines, "What's My Rule?" tables, and Frames-and-Arrows diagrams. | ● | ● | ● | ◐ | ● | ● | ● | ◐ | ● | ○ |
| [**Patterns, Functions, and Algebra Goal 2**] Read, write, and explain expressions and number sentences using the symbols +, −, and = and the symbols > and < with cues; solve equations involving addition and subtraction. | ○ | ● | ● | ○ | ● | ● | ● | ● | ● | ○ |

Unit column header: **Unit**

# Maintaining Concepts and Skills

Some of the goals addressed in this unit will be addressed again in Unit 10. Those goals marked with an asterisk (*) are addressed in Unit 10 only as practice and application. Here are several suggestions for maintaining concepts and skills.

## Number and Numeration Goal 4*

◆ Have children match fractions to circles divided into fractional parts. See the Readiness activity in Lesson 9-7 for more information.

## Operations and Computation Goal 2

◆ Have children play *Beat the Calculator* and *Addition Top-It*.

◆ Have children use base-10 blocks to solve 2-digit addition and subtraction problems. See the Readiness activity in Lesson 9-4 for more information.

## Patterns, Functions, and Algebra Goal 1*

◆ Have children assemble a number grid from separate pieces. See the Readiness activity in Lesson 9-1 for more information.

◆ Have children play *Pin the Number on the Number Grid.* See the Readiness activity in Lesson 9-3 for more information.

◆ Have children use the "What's My Rule?" master on page 130 of this handbook to create practice problems.

## Patterns, Functions, and Algebra Goal 2*

◆ Have children play the *Digit Game* and for each round record their number and their partner's number with $>$ , $<$ , or $=$ placed correctly between the two numbers.

# Assessment

See page 120 in the *Assessment Handbook* for modifications to the written portion of the Unit 9 Progress Check.

Additionally, see pages 121–125 for modifications to the open-response task and selected child work samples.

# Activities and Ideas for Differentiation

In this unit, children review many of the key concepts developed during the year including linear measurement, data, time, and arithmetic. This section summarizes opportunities for supporting multiple learning styles and ability levels. Use these suggestions to develop a differentiation plan for Unit 10.

## Part 1 Activities That Support Differentiation

Below are examples of Unit 10 activities that highlight some of the general instructional strategies that are hallmarks of a differentiated classroom. These strategies will help you support, emphasize, and enhance lesson content to make sure all your children are engaged in the mathematics at the highest possible level. For more information about general differentiation strategies that accommodate the diverse needs of today's classrooms, see the essay on pages 8–16 of this handbook.

| Lesson | Activity | Strategy |
|--------|----------|----------|
| 10◆1 | Children make a line plot of their height data using stick-on notes and find the middle value. | Modeling physically |
| 10◆2 | Children show times on their tool-kit clocks. | Modeling concretely |
| 10◆3 | Children use coins to act out vending-machine purchases. | Modeling concretely |
| 10◆5 | Children construct polygons with straws and twist-ties to compare the polygons' properties. | Modeling concretely |
| 10◆6 | Use the Class Thermometer Poster to compare temperatures. | Using a visual reference |
| 10◆7 | Children model numbers with base-10 blocks. | Modeling concretely |

## Vocabulary Development

The lessons of Unit 10 build on student understanding of the vocabulary in previous units; no new vocabulary is introduced. Encourage students to use their mathematics vocabulary regularly and review any words or phrases that continue to cause difficulty.

Lessons include suggestions for helping English language learners understand and develop vocabulary. For more information, see pages 17–19 of this handbook.

 **Games**

Below are suggested Unit 10 game adaptations. For more information about implementing games in a differentiated classroom, see pages 20–25 of this handbook.

**Game: *Beat the Calculator***

Skill Practiced: **Solve addition problems.** [Operations and Computation Goal 2]

| Modification | Purpose of Modification |
|---|---|
| The caller rolls two 6-sided dice instead of using cards. | Children solve addition problems for addends less than 7. [Operations and Computation Goal 2] |
| The caller draws two number cards. The first card becomes a multiple of 10 (a 2 becomes 20). The second card is the subtrahend and is subtracted from the first. If the caller draws 3 and 7. The problem is 30 – 7. | Children solve subtraction problems with 2-digit minuends and 1-digit subtrahends. [Operations and Computation Goal 2] |

**Game: *Coin-Dice Game***

Skill Practiced: **Make coin exchanges.** [Measurement and Reference Frames Goal 2]

| Modification | Purpose of Modification |
|---|---|
| Players use only pennies and nickels. | Children make coin exchanges for pennies and nickels. [Measurement and Reference Frames Goal 2] |
| Players use number cards 1–20 (four each of 1–10 and one each of 11–20). With each turn, they pick up a coin combination that is worth the number on the card. They get a bonus penny if they pick up the combination using the fewest possible coins. | Children make coin combinations and coin exchanges. [Operations and Computation Goal 2; Measurement and Reference Frames Goal 2] |

**Game: *$1, $10, $100 Exchange Game***

Skill Practiced: **Exchange $1, $10, and $100 bills.** [Measurement and Reference Frames Goal 2]

| Modification | Purpose of Modification |
|---|---|
| Players use a bank of thirty $10 bills and one $100 bill. They roll one die on each turn and collect that number of $10 bills. The first player to get two $100 bills wins. | Children exchange ten $10 bills for a $100 bill. [Measurement and Reference Frames Goal 2] |
| The bank starts with one $1,000 bank draft, twenty $100 bills, twenty $10 bills, and twenty $1 bills. Players use number cards 1–20 (four each of 1–10 and one each of 11–20). On each turn, they take a combination of bills for the total value on the card. The winner is the first player to collect a bank draft. | Children exchange $1, $10, and $100 bills. They finally exchange for a $1,000 bank draft. [Measurement and Reference Frames Goal 2] |

 **Math Boxes**

Suggestions for using Math Boxes to meet individual needs begin on page 26 of this handbook. There are blank masters for Math Boxes on pages 120–125.

# Using Part 3 of the Lessons

Use your professional judgment, along with assessment results, to determine whether the whole class, small groups, or individual children might benefit from these Unit 10 activities. Consider using the Part 3 Planning Master found on page 138 of this handbook to record your plans.

## Readiness Activities

| Lesson | Activity | Purpose of Activity |
|---|---|---|
| 10◆1 | Tell and solve number stories using animal-length cards. | Gain experience calculating differences. [Operations and Computation Goal 2] |
| 10◆2 | Match digital times to times on an analog clock. | Explore telling time. [Measurement and Reference Frames Goal 4] |
| 10◆3 | Count collections of quarters, dimes, and nickels and determine the total value of the coins. | Gain experience counting coin combinations. [Operations and Computation Goal 2] |
| 10◆4 | Compare quantities of pennies using one-to-one correspondence. | Explore comparing quantities. [Number and Numeration Goal 7] |
| 10◆5 | Play *I Spy* with 2- and 3-dimensional shapes. | Gain experience with attributes of 2- and 3-dimensional shapes. [Geometry Goal 1] |
| 10◆6 | Find the difference between 2-digit numbers on a number grid. | Explore finding differences. [Operations and Computation Goal 2] |
| 10◆7 | Use base-10 blocks to build numbers and identify missing digits. | Explore place value. [Number and Numeration Goal 3] |

## English Language Learners Support Activities

| Lesson | Activity | Purpose of Activity |
|---|---|---|
| 10◆4 | Add *change* and *making change* to the Math Word Bank. | Make connections among and use visuals to represent terms. [Operations and Computation Goal 2] |
| 10◆5 | Use shape words and pictures to compare 2- and 3-dimensional shapes. | Make connections between terms and visual models [Geometry Goal 1] |
| 10◆6 | Add *thermometer* and *weather* to the Math Word Bank. | Make connections among and use visuals to represent terms. [Measurement and Reference Frames Goal 3] |

## Enrichment Activities

| Lesson | Activity | Purpose of Activity |
|---|---|---|
| 10◆1 | Collect data about calculator counts. | Explore data collections. [Data and Chance Goal 1] |
| 10◆2 | Use tool-kit clocks to determine elapsed time. | Apply understanding of time concepts. [Measurement and Reference Frames Goal 4] |
| 10◆4 | Write and solve money number stories using advertisements. | Apply understanding number stories. [Operations and Computation Goal 4] |
| 10◆5 | Construct polyhedrons with straws and twist-ties. | Explore the properties of 3-dimensional figures. [Geometry Goal 1] |
| 10◆6 | Compare the Celsius scale to the Fahrenheit scale on a thermometer. | Explore temperature. [Measurement and Reference Frames Goal 3] |
| 10◆7 | Write 3-digit numbers in expanded notation. | Apply understanding of place value. [Number and Numeration Goal 3] |

## Extra Practice Activities

| Lesson | Activity | Purpose of Activity |
|---|---|---|
| 10◆2 | Read *It's About Time, Max!*; draw an activity and tell what time the activity occurs. | Practice telling time on an analog clock. [Measurement and Reference Frames Goal 4] |
| 10◆3 | Play the *Coin-Dice Game.* | Practice making coin exchanges. [Measurement and Reference Frames Goal 2] |
| 10◆4 | Play *Dime-Nickel-Penny Grab.* | Practice making money exchanges. [Measurement and Reference Frames Goal 2] |
| 10◆6 | Find temperature differences on a thermometer in *Minute Math*+ activities. | Practice with temperature. [Measurement and Reference Frames Goal 3] |

# Looking at Grade-Level Goals

*Everyday Mathematics* develops concepts and skills over time. Below is a chart showing where the Grade-Level Goals emphasized in this unit are addressed throughout the year. Use the chart to help you determine which Maintaining Concepts and Skills activities on page 118 to utilize to ensure that children continue working toward these Grade-Level Goals.

- ● Grade-Level Goal is taught.
- ◐ Grade-Level Goal is practiced.
- ○ Grade-Level Goal is not a focus.

| Grade-Level Goals Emphasized in Unit 10 | 1 | 2 | 3 | 4 | 5 | 6 | 7 | 8 | 9 | 10 |
|---|---|---|---|---|---|---|---|---|---|---|
| [Number and Numeration Goal 1] Count on by 1s, 2s, 5s, and 10s past 100 and back by 1s from any number less than 100 with and without number grids, number lines, and calculators. | ● | ● | ● | ● | ● | ● | ◐ | ◐ | ● | ● |
| [Operations and Computation Goal 2] Use manipulatives, number grids, tally marks, mental arithmetic, and calculators to solve problems involving the addition and subtraction of 1- or 2-digit whole numbers with 1- or 2-digit whole numbers; calculate and compare the values of combinations of coins. | ● | ● | ● | ● | ● | ● | ◐ | ● | ● | ● |
| [Operations and Computation Goal 4] Identify change-to-more, change-to-less, comparison, and parts-and-total situations. | ○ | ○ | ○ | ◐ | ● | ○ | ◐ | ● | ◐ | ● |

# Maintaining Concepts and Skills

After completing the curriculum, here are several suggestions for maintaining and practicing concepts and skills.

### Number and Numeration Goal 1

◆ Have children use the Number-Grid master on page 132 of this handbook to shade skip-counting patterns.

### Operations and Computation Goal 1

◆ Have children play *Beat the Calculator* with easy facts.

### Operations and Computation Goal 2

◆ Have children tell and solve number stories using animal-length cards. See the Readiness activity in Lesson 10-1 for more information.

◆ Have children count collections of coins. See the Readiness activity in Lesson 10-3 for more information.

### Measurement and Reference Frames Goal 2

◆ Have children play different versions of exchange games—*Coin Exchange; Penny-Dime-Dollar Exchange; $1, $10, $100 Exchange.*

### Measurement and Reference Frames Goal 4

◆ Have children play *Time Match.*

### Patterns, Functions, and Algebra Goal 1

◆ Have children play the *Attribute Train Game.*

◆ Use Frames-and-Arrows masters A and B on pages 128 and 129 of this handbook to create practice problems.

◆ Use the "What's My Rule?" master on page 130 of this handbook to create practice problems.

## Assessment

See page 128 in the *Assessment Handbook* for modifications to the written portion of the Unit 10 Progress Check.

Additionally, see pages 129–133 for modifications to the open-response task and selected child work samples.

# Masters

The masters listed below provide additional resources that you can customize to meet the needs of a diverse group of learners. The templates, pages 120–137, include additional Math Boxes problem sets, more practice with program routines, and support for language development. Use the Part 3 Planning Master, page 138, to record information about your differentiation plan.

## Contents

**Masters**

# Math Boxes A

**1.**

**2.**

**3.**

**4.**

# Math Boxes B

**1.**

**2.**

**3.**

**4.**

**5.**

**6.**

# Math Boxes C

**1.**

**2.**

in

| in | out |
|----|-----|
|    |     |
|    |     |
|    |     |
|    |     |
|    |     |
|    |     |
|    |     |

Rule

out

**3.**

Rule

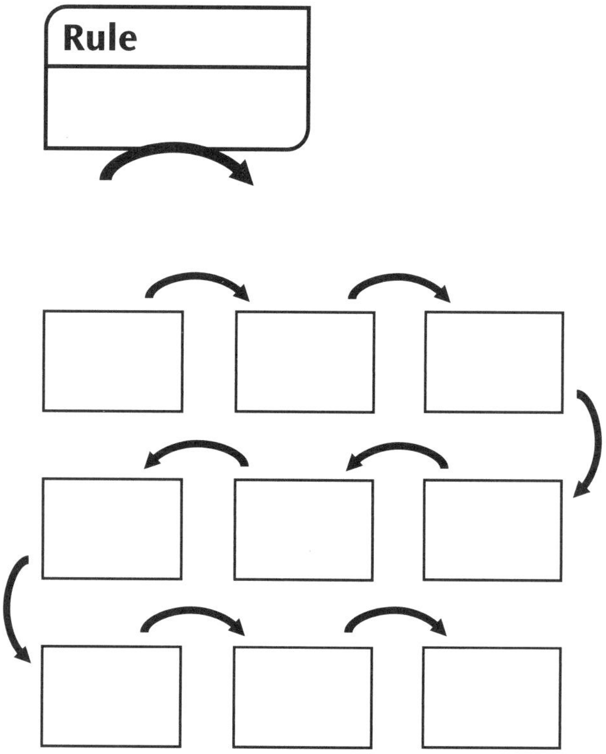

**4.** Complete the number-grid puzzle.

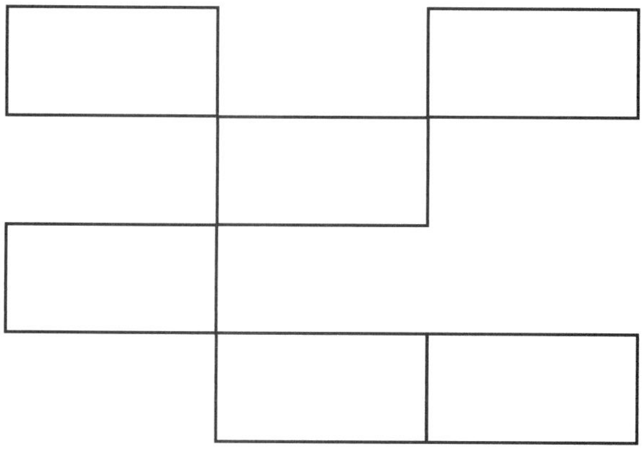

# Math Boxes D

**1.** Write the time for

____ **:** ____

**2.** Use words or pictures to tell a number story.

| Unit |
| --- |
|  |

**3.** Write the numbers that come next.

☐ , ____ , ____

☐ , ____ , ____

☐ , ____ , ____

**4.** Write the number that comes before.

____ , ☐

____ , ☐

____ , ☐

# Math Boxes E

**1.** Use Ⓟ, Ⓝ, Ⓓ, and Ⓠ to

show _____ ¢.

**2.** Use words or pictures to tell a number story.

| Unit |
|------|
|      |

**3.** Draw the hands to show

_____ : _____.

**4.** Write a fact family for the domino.

_____

_____

_____

_____

# Math Boxes F

**1.**

Rule

**2.** Count back by

_____ s.

| Start |

____ , ____ , ____

____ , ____ , ____

**3.** Write the time for

_____ : _____

**4.** Write the number that is

_____ more.

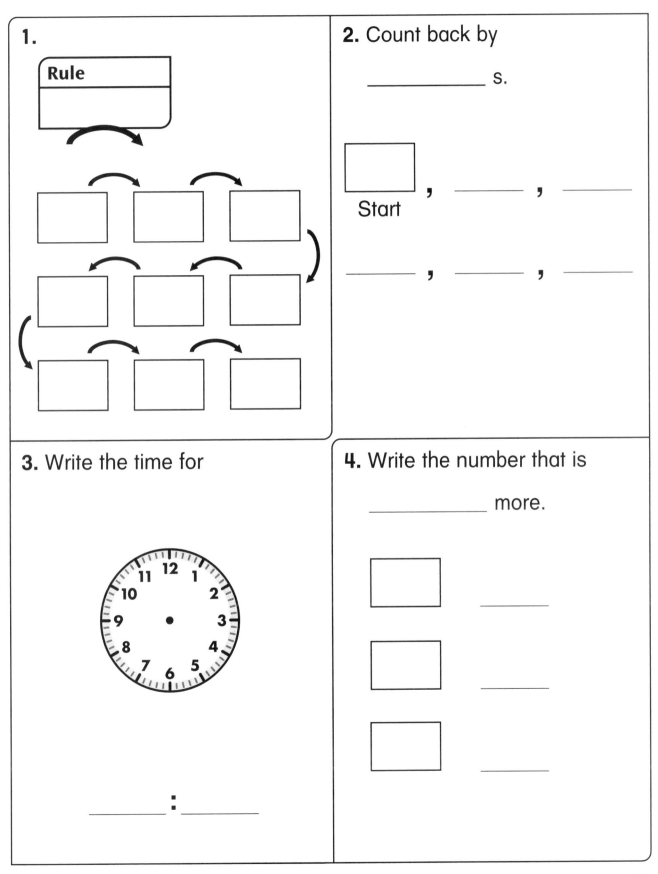

# Math Word Bank A

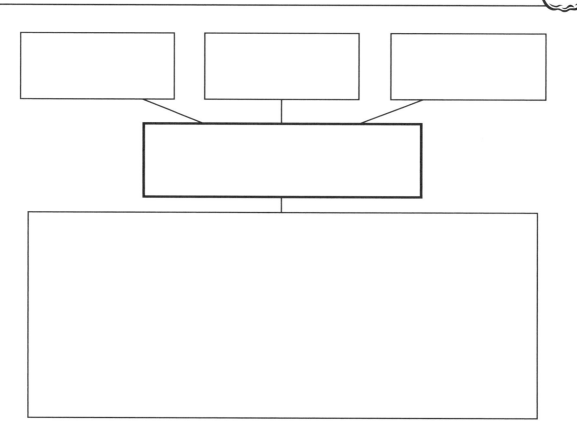

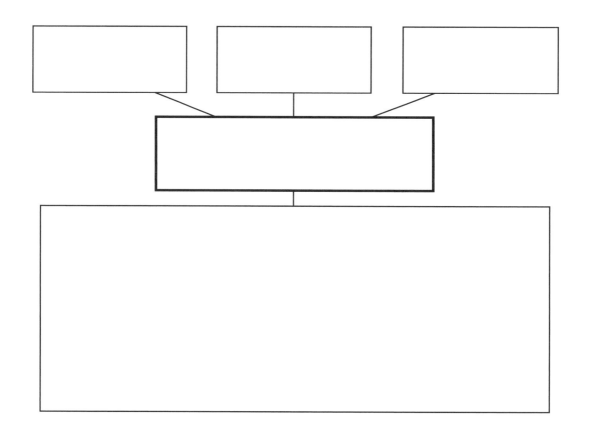

# Math Word Bank B

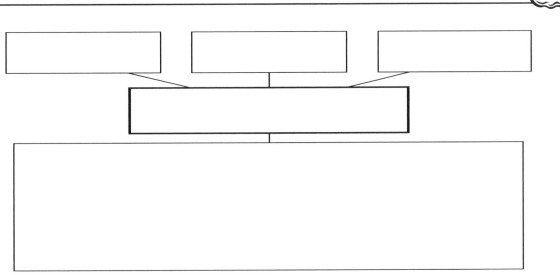

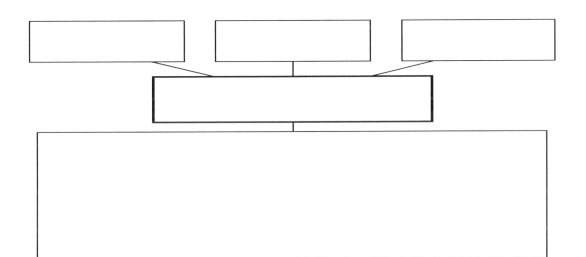

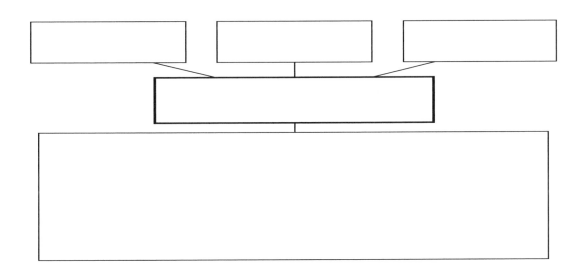

# Frames and Arrows A

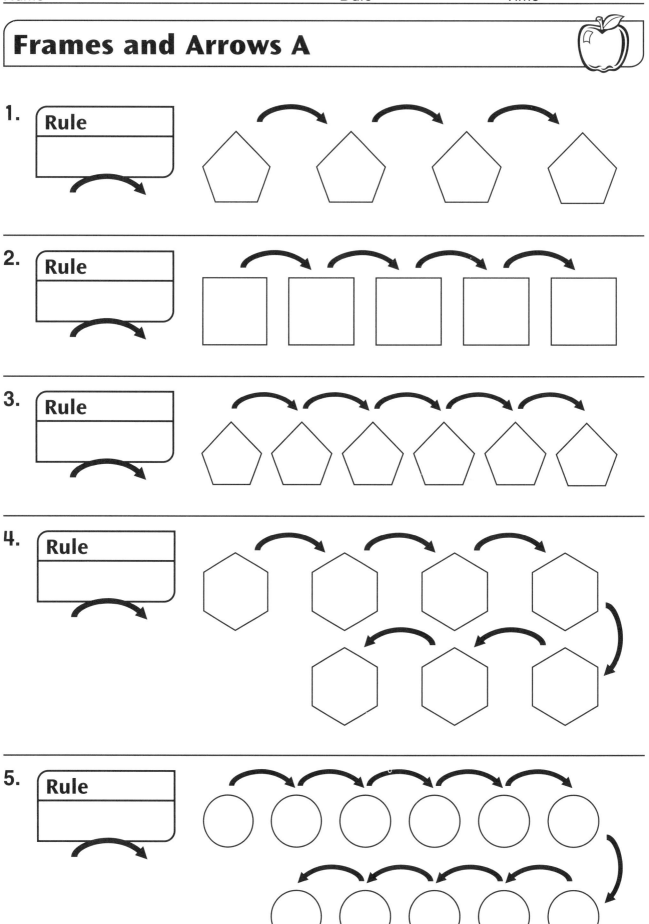

1. Rule

2. Rule

3. Rule

4. Rule

5. Rule

# Frames and Arrows B

**1.**

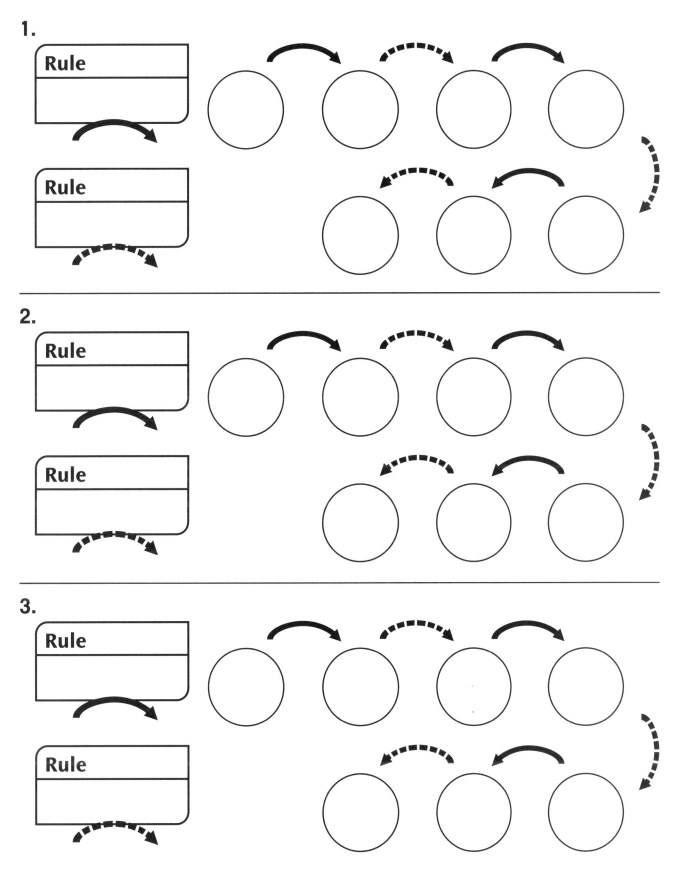

**2.**

**3.**

# "What's My Rule?"

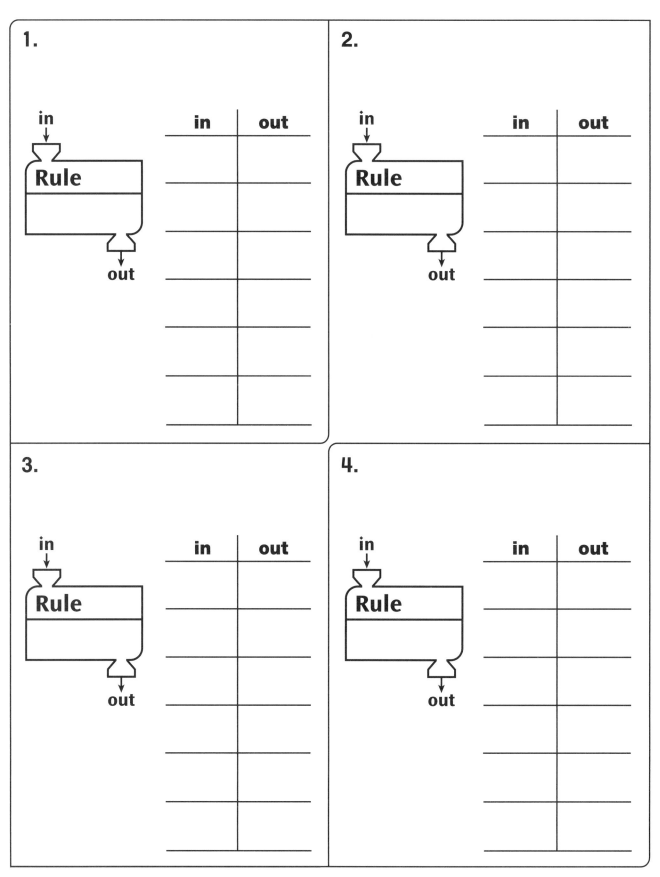

**1.**

in

| Rule |
|------|

out

| in | out |
|----|-----|
|    |     |
|    |     |
|    |     |
|    |     |
|    |     |
|    |     |

**2.**

in

| Rule |
|------|

out

| in | out |
|----|-----|
|    |     |
|    |     |
|    |     |
|    |     |
|    |     |
|    |     |

**3.**

in

| Rule |
|------|

out

| in | out |
|----|-----|
|    |     |
|    |     |
|    |     |
|    |     |
|    |     |

**4.**

in

| Rule |
|------|

out

| in | out |
|----|-----|
|    |     |
|    |     |
|    |     |
|    |     |
|    |     |

# Name-Collection Boxes

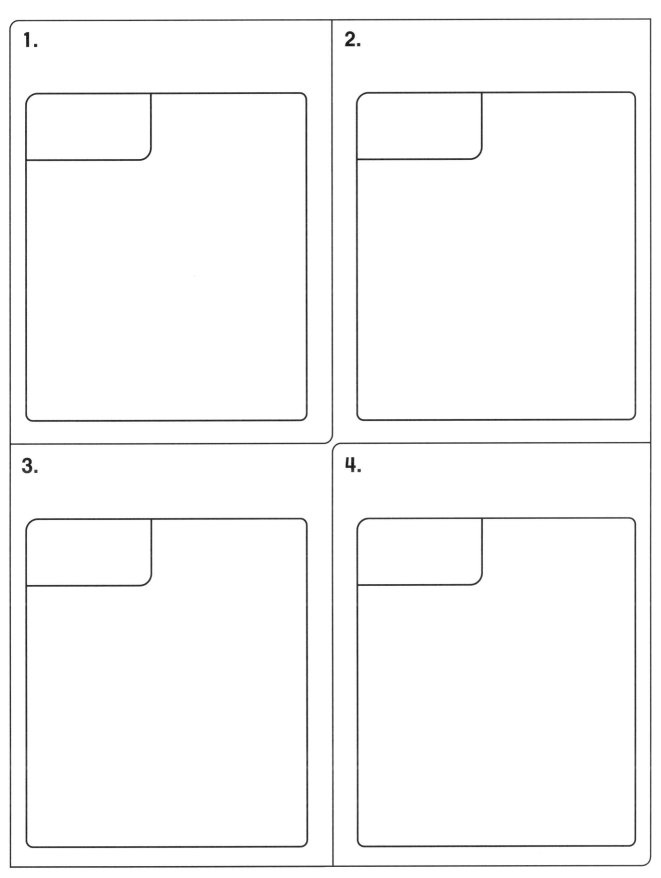

1.

2.

3.

4.

# Number Grid

| −9 | −8 | −7 | −6 | −5 | −4 | −3 | −2 | −1 | 0 |
|---|---|---|---|---|---|---|---|---|---|
| 1 | 2 | 3 | 4 | 5 | 6 | 7 | 8 | 9 | 10 |
| 11 | 12 | 13 | 14 | 15 | 16 | 17 | 18 | 19 | 20 |
| 21 | 22 | 23 | 24 | 25 | 26 | 27 | 28 | 29 | 30 |
| 31 | 32 | 33 | 34 | 35 | 36 | 37 | 38 | 39 | 40 |
| 41 | 42 | 43 | 44 | 45 | 46 | 47 | 48 | 49 | 50 |
| 51 | 52 | 53 | 54 | 55 | 56 | 57 | 58 | 59 | 60 |
| 61 | 62 | 63 | 64 | 65 | 66 | 67 | 68 | 69 | 70 |
| 71 | 72 | 73 | 74 | 75 | 76 | 77 | 78 | 79 | 80 |
| 81 | 82 | 83 | 84 | 85 | 86 | 87 | 88 | 89 | 90 |
| 91 | 92 | 93 | 94 | 95 | 96 | 97 | 98 | 99 | 100 |
| 101 | 102 | 103 | 104 | 105 | 106 | 107 | 108 | 109 | 110 |

| −9 | −8 | −7 | −6 | −5 | −4 | −3 | −2 | −1 | 0 |
|---|---|---|---|---|---|---|---|---|---|
| 1 | 2 | 3 | 4 | 5 | 6 | 7 | 8 | 9 | 10 |
| 11 | 12 | 13 | 14 | 15 | 16 | 17 | 18 | 19 | 20 |
| 21 | 22 | 23 | 24 | 25 | 26 | 27 | 28 | 29 | 30 |
| 31 | 32 | 33 | 34 | 35 | 36 | 37 | 38 | 39 | 40 |
| 41 | 42 | 43 | 44 | 45 | 46 | 47 | 48 | 49 | 50 |
| 51 | 52 | 53 | 54 | 55 | 56 | 57 | 58 | 59 | 60 |
| 61 | 62 | 63 | 64 | 65 | 66 | 67 | 68 | 69 | 70 |
| 71 | 72 | 73 | 74 | 75 | 76 | 77 | 78 | 79 | 80 |
| 81 | 82 | 83 | 84 | 85 | 86 | 87 | 88 | 89 | 90 |
| 91 | 92 | 93 | 94 | 95 | 96 | 97 | 98 | 99 | 100 |
| 101 | 102 | 103 | 104 | 105 | 106 | 107 | 108 | 109 | 110 |

# Venn Diagram A

# Venn Diagram B

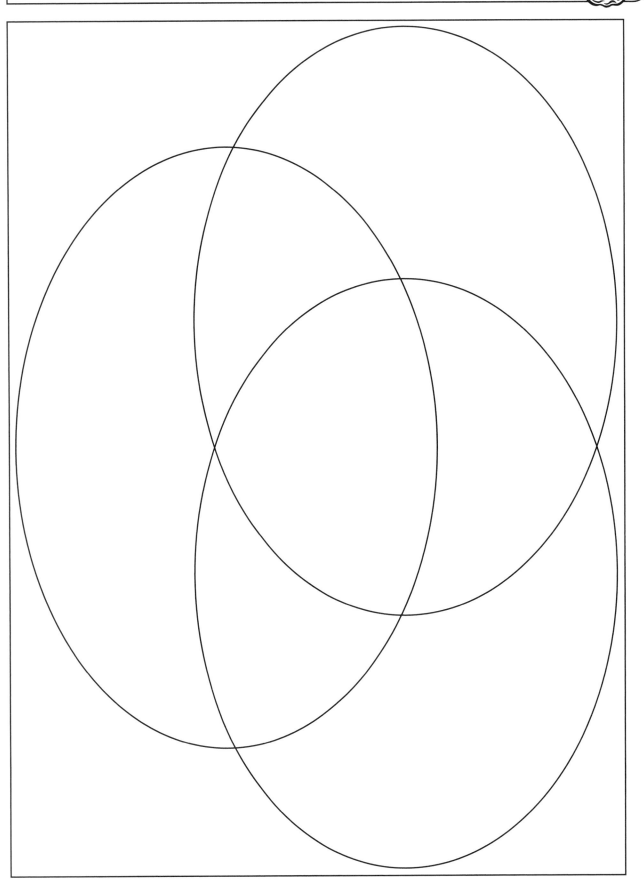

# Situation Diagrams for Number Stories

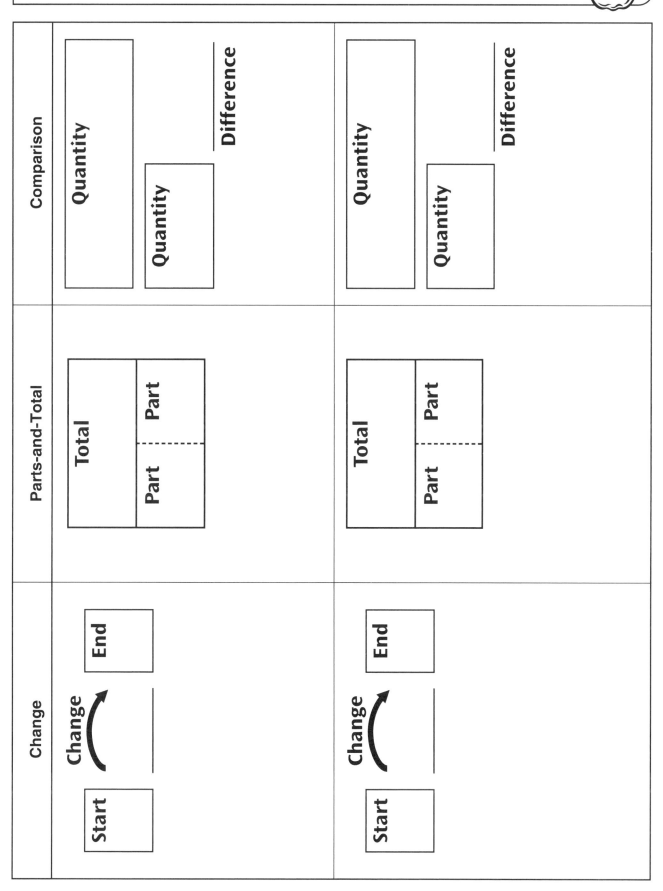

# Multiplication/Division Diagrams

| | | |
|---|---|---|
| _____ | _____<br>per _____ | _____ in all |
| | | |

| | | |
|---|---|---|
| _____ | _____<br>per _____ | _____ in all |
| | | |

| | | |
|---|---|---|
| _____ | _____<br>per _____ | _____ in all |
| | | |

# Home Link

# Part 3 Planning Master

| Lesson | Readiness | Enrichment | Extra Practice | ELL Support |
|---|---|---|---|---|
| | | | | |
| | | | | |
| | | | | |
| | | | | |
| | | | | |
| | | | | |
| | | | | |

# Resources

## Recommended Reading

Baxter, Juliet A., John Woodward, and Deborah Olson. 2001. "Effects of Reform-Based Mathematics Instruction on Low Achievers in Five Third-Grade Classrooms." *The Elementary School Journal* 101 (5): 529–547.

Garnett, Kate. 1998. "Math Learning Disabilities." LD OnLine. www.ldonline.org (accessed Jan. 19, 2004).

Johnson, Dana T. 2000. "Teaching Mathematics to Gifted Students in a Mixed-Ability Classroom." Reston, Va.: ERIC Clearinghouse on Disabilities and Gifted Education.

Lock, Robin H. 1996. "Adapting Mathematics Instruction in the General Education Classroom for Students with Mathematics Disabilities." LD OnLine. www.ldonline.org (accessed Jan. 19, 2004).

Tomlinson, Carol Ann. 1999. *The Differentiated Classroom: Responding to the Needs of All Learners.* Alexandria, Va.: Association for Supervision & Curriculum Development.

Usiskin, Zalman. 1994. "Individual Differences in the Teaching and Learning of Mathematics." Chicago, Ill.: UCSMP Newsletter 14 (Winter).

Villa, Richard A., and Jacqueline S. Thousand, eds. 1995. *Creating an Inclusive School.* Alexandria, Va.: Association for Supervision & Curriculum Development.

http://everydaymath.uchicago.edu/

## References

Gregory, Gayle H. 2003. *Differentiated Instructional Strategies in Practice: Training, Implementation, and Supervision.* Thousand Oaks, Calif.: Corwin Press.

Robertson, Connie, ed. 1998. *Dictionary of Quotations (Wordsworth Reference Series).* 3rd Rev. Edition. Hertfordshire, UK: Wordsworth Editions Ltd.

Tomlinson, Carol Ann. 2003. "Deciding to Teach Them All." *Educational Leadership* 61 (2): 6–11.